WHO'D PLANT

Who'd Plant a Church?

DIANA ARCHER

CHRISTINA PRESS
CROWBOROUGH, EAST SUSSEX

British Library Cataloguing Data
A catalogue record for this book is available
from the British Library.

ISBN 1 901387 06 2

Designed and produced by Bookprint Creative Services
P.O. Box 827, BN21 3YJ, England for
CHRISTINA PRESS LTD
Highland House, Aviemore Road
Crowborough, East Sussex, TN6 1QX.
Printed in Great Britain.

For Both My Dads

Contents

Acknowledgements

What can I say? Without the people of Cavendish Community Church, Felixstowe, this book could not have been written. My passionate thanks to all of you—those named in these pages, and those not—you are all here anyway. You have given me the experience of a lifetime.

A special mention to Joan for her careful chronology, Lesley for her typing, Keith for his encouragement and prayer, David W. Griggs for his wonderful drawings.

Undying thanks to my sister Pam Macnaughton for her excellent editing and belief in me. And of course, gratitude unbounding to my husband who bore the brunt of it all, and my children who are the best ever.

Thanks be, especially, to God.

Foreword

What an adventure! Starting a church from scratch. The story told in this fascinating book begins with a young couple, two small children, a half-built vicarage on a new estate and a triangular plot of ground where a new church might be built one day. As I read Chapter 1, I thought, 'Wow! Just think of it, no one to say, "But we do it like that here at St. . . ." No robed choir to glare at a vicar who dares to mention Graham Kendrick; no rigid rows of pews to hamper spontaneous worship, and no ancient organist who's been around so long he must have met Charles Wesley.'

No new churches are ever planted in a 'bed of roses'. Diana tells us how it felt to have these 'God-searching folk' from the estate arriving for a service in her newly furnished lounge and then spilling a stream of coffee over the lovely pink carpet. And although a 7 am prayer meeting did seem like an excellent idea, it was not so good when the 'vicarage' overslept and left the 'faithful' hammering on the front door.

Yes, cramming thirty people into your home for a service every Sunday was probably no joke, nor as the numbers increased. The baby church had to learn to survive in the 'nomad syndrome' which consists of an endless search for suitable premises, the inevitable packing and unpacking of equipment and rearranging moulded, plastic stacking chairs.

To save you cheating and taking a peep at the last chapter, yes they get their lovely new building up on that triangle of land – eventually. But so much has to happen first, not only to the ever-expanding congregation but also inside the vicarage itself. It is being allowed to walk in behind that front door which makes this book so well worth reading. This is not just the story of a developing church but also a developing vicar – not to mention his wife! Diana writes one rather poignant paragraph which stands out in my memory.

> Strange dynamics fly around the person of the church leader.
> . . . We each need different things in a leader. . . . Teacher,
> preacher, shepherd, counsellor, carer, initiator, comforter,
> social worker, problem solver, figurehead, prophet . . . a
> leader may be all these things in some measure, at some time
> . . . but no one can be just what different people would like
> all the time. So there will be hurt . . . disappointment . . . dis-
> illusionment. . . . It is very hard to be the focus of that. If
> people do not like you, they are likely to leave. If everybody
> left there would be no church. There is a subtle pressure here
> then to be likeable and to want to please. To forget it is God
> who builds churches, actually.

Graham and Diana have to ask themselves, 'Who are we trying to please, our new little flock or God?' and 'Why does it matter so much not to let someone down?' These are the issues the vicarage family are forced to face. As we watch these two struggling with the motives which drive them, most of us who serve God in any capacity will probably feel we need to ask ourselves the same questions. 'Why we do it anyway?'

I first met Diana at a conference where I was speaking to the wives of church leaders. Some of the pain they were able to express in that safe place was horrible to watch. How is it that we Christians can be so cruel to each other? I think we are suffering an epidemic at the moment. I call it 'clergy battering' and it cuts across all denominations. For some obscure reason we all feel we have the right to tear our leaders apart with criticism and then kick the severed bits around the congregations for sport. It may be fun for those of us in the pews, but it's no laughing matter behind the front door of the vicarage or manse. I will never forget those tear-stained faces Diana and I observed as the leader's wives shared with us some of the things which had been said or done by congregations to their husbands.

Diana has bravely refused to write this book from the top of a pedestal. She has been so remarkably honest about their 'warts' and failings that we pew-fillers could even get the impression that the clergy were ordinary human beings like the rest of us.

This book will inspire those who are in the business of helping God to plant a new church, but I hope it will also give the rest of us some insights into the costs involved in doing so.

Jennifer Rees Larcombe

Not me, Lord!

'But nobody will come!' I wailed. 'We'll be fasting and praying for months on end. Just you, me and two kids.'

The sharp sea wind snatched at my words, tossing them carelessly into the air.

I shivered.

'No house, no church, no people. I just can't do it.' Angrily I jerked my windswept hair out of my eyes as I looked up to follow my husband's gaze. Massive billowing clouds clamoured for my attention as they turned spectacular shades of red and gold. Bother. God knows I love sunsets. Surely he wasn't trying to encourage me through this one?

'If it's the right thing for us to do—then we do it.' Graham sounded certain, but I wasn't convinced.

We collected two reluctant children from the swings, and wandered back to the car. The sunset colours bounced off the sea and demanded attention again. Silently we drove away, wrestling with our thoughts. How could it be right for us, for me? I suppose that over the four years my husband had been a curate I had learned to enjoy being a clergy wife in the sort of church which placed no expectations on me and left me free to do my own thing. The people were warm, loving and caring.

People. That, of course, was the problem. If we came to begin a new church—a church plant—we didn't know if there ever would be any people. My husband's future boss had driven us round the housing estate by the sea and indicated that our potential congregation could be lurking behind each closed door. He was trying to be encouraging, I knew, but then *he* wasn't the one being asked to come.

I suppose it was the house that helped to change my mind. On that half-built, church-less housing estate, there was only one new house rising from the ground. It was right in the middle. It was just near the donated site for a possible church building. It wasn't spoken for, and it was at the stage where a few minor adjustments—like the addition of a study—could be made to accommodate a man working from home. So I had to admit that events were conspiring against me, and God seemed to be nudging me on.

However I still did not *want* to go, and the house didn't make it feel any better. We were still only a church of four. That we would stay that way remained my biggest fear.

I don't really know how to describe what happened next. The house was finished and we moved in. By now there were completed houses beside us and a building site opposite. A small article appeared in the local paper about a vicar without a church. Said vicar seemed to be excited about the future. Said vicar's wife was just dead nervous. The whole of the next few years depended on whether a church materialised. Never before had I understood so well that the church is the people, not the building.

I reckoned without our previous church though. One sunny Saturday, down they poured in carloads, spilling out onto the streets, bringing puppets and drama, flyers and music, balloons and enthusiasm. Letterboxes flapped and children gathered as the news spread. Something was going on! So there was quite a crowd for our first open-air service on the green opposite the swings that afternoon. There was music, and the mayor, and the Bishop . . . and a sense of excitement. Even I couldn't deny that. It ended with my husband inviting all and sundry to a shared tea and family service in our lounge in eight days time.

Those eight days must have been some of the longest in my life. But when 4.30 pm came, we cleared back the furniture, put on the kettle and opened the door.

'Hallo. Nice to meet you. Please come in.'

I said it thirty-six times.

I couldn't believe it. People! Big people, precious little

15

people. Tall people, short people; shy people, friendly people. Wonderful people, all of them! People coming, when I thought there would be none. People for God to mould together into a family. People to learn to love. People to begin a church. People for an adventure. . . .

1

The Startling Grace of God

The little boy was crying again. A jumble of half-packed cardboard boxes littered the kitchen, and the kettle lead had disappeared. That nightmare, 'we're-never-going-to-make-it' feeling was threatening to engulf me as I turned to wash hands smeared with newspaper print before picking up my two-year-old son.

'I still can't believe we're doing this,' I sighed to my friend Siân, as she reached to clear a top shelf of old tins, long past their sell-by date.

'It's all a big blank,' I added.

Suddenly the four years of curacy for my husband at St Matthew's, Ipswich seemed frighteningly brief as I contemplated the unknown future. Despite the inevitable heartaches, mistakes and problems, it had been such a good time of learning and growing. We'd seen many areas of the church expand, and gained some precious friendships. The thought of leaving everybody and everything made me feel wobbly inside, and scared too. 'God is always leading us out from security to insecurity, wanting us to trust him when there's nothing else.' How often had I listened to David Meikle, my vicar and my husband's boss, challenging our faith with this, one of his favourite themes. It was easy to sit in the relative safety of a large established church and nod in agreement. Now, faced with the reality of being a living illustration, it all felt a bit much.

'There, that's another box done.' Siân's voice cut across my rising panic. 'Aren't you raring to go then?'

'No I am not!' I retorted, hugging my son rather fiercely. 'How would you feel going to a non-existent church with no people?'

'Well at least your house is in the right place,' she reminded me.

I sighed. 'Just now it seems more important that it will be opposite the supermarket.' I had much faith that the convenient shop would appear, but only a mustard seed of belief for a church.

I took a deep breath.

'I guess all we've got is the conviction that God wants us to go.' It was slowly said. 'That's what I've got to hang on to. There just isn't anything else.'

So it was with fear and trembling, and a feeling of unreality that we finally moved all our wordly goods—never did find the kettle lead—and ourselves to Felixstowe in July 1989. I tried to hide my uncertainty from five-year-old Judith and little Paul. But they were excited exploring the new, larger house and hardly noticed their definitely dazed mum. Time raced by as we investigated schools, doctors, dentists, shops, the beach . . . and the open-air service day was upon us. Credit where it's due—my husband was great that day, as he readied for the challenge of building a church from nought. *I* had my hands full trying to persuade Paul not to wear his sister's bracelet and hairband for the big occasion. I failed. So the photographs . . . he really *is* a boy!

Talking of clothes, Graham had some decisions to make before the following Sunday. Looking back, it was a good thing he kept his slippers on. Those and his casual jumper seemed a far cry from the Sunday black and white of cassock and surplice, but as we opened our door and our lives to those first thirty-six, it seemed to put them at ease. Anyway, I guess priestly garb would have blocked the corridors. Certainly it would have got splashed with tea or smeared with chocolate cake as our visitors piled into the kitchen and dining room with offerings for the shared meal, and I flicked the kettle switch again and again—got a new lead. Utterly surprised, I rummaged in newly-filled cupboards for yet more mugs as I attempted to commit some names and faces to memory. Had God really brought all these people on our very first door-opening Sunday?

Bemused joy brought an unrestrainable smile to my face as we settled in our moderately-sized pink lounge for our first informal family service, extra chairs squashed in, children on laps and the floor. A collection of safe songs— oldies but goodies, which a fair few seemed to know— accompanied by Graham's guitar; Bible readings; prayers for all to join if they wanted to, and a bit of chat from slipper man. Nothing too threatening, yet there they were, people gathering in God's name: the intrigued, fascinated by the idea of a vicar without a church; the brave, Christians looking for a new start; the supportive, those happy to share their time from their town churches to help us get off the ground; and then somehow most precious, the specials, attracted by the atmosphere of the open-air service and wanting to find out more.

After all the goodbyes had been said and we flopped down on our lounge chairs—still in rows—our minds were buzzing with faces, names and ideas. A source of cheap mugs seemed of paramount importance, not to mention a tidy garage. Fortunately the latter was within our grasp as we hadn't had time to fill it with our usual junk, just leftover packing cases. Hubby was definitely encouraged as he started enthusing about next Sunday.

'OK, we'll stick to the 4.30 afternoon tea and service idea,' he decided. 'It seemed to work and doesn't clash with the town churches. But the children need something just for them, so I'll haul them off to the garage while the grown-ups finish tea.'

And so the Den Gang was born.

That night as we collapsed exhausted into bed, I was filled with amazement and not a little relief at such an unexpected beginning. Maybe we were in the right place after all. Yet when I looked ahead to the challenge of the totally unknown in the coming weeks, I was aware of a mesmerising mixture of fear and excitement as I wondered what God would do, all on his own, as it were. I'd seen him operate through churches of many different traditions—but he'd had plenty of support there, hadn't he? Now it was just very-human us, and a house. Nothing else. No history, no back-up, no colleagues. I think I was also wondering whether I and my limited faith would cope. . . .

Our second Sunday, and this time we approached it with more anticipation. We'd gained a name—Cavendish Community Church—picked on the spur of the moment when filling in a form for a Billy Graham rally. It seemed appropriate, being on the Cavendish Park estates and certainly dependent on the community for a raison d'être. We'd also had several visitors to our front door, coming to pledge their encouragement and support, which was wonderful.

Here it came again, Sunday door-opening time. Our second round saw just twenty-two over the threshold, carefully counted, and I had a little wobble. Was it all going to fizzle out before it started? Where were the others? Did we do something wrong? Yet the atmosphere felt relaxed and good. There was no chance of standing on ceremony while squeezing past each other in the ungenerous corridor, washing up together, or retrieving scones and jam from the carpet.

Both Graham and I remembered some names, which was a miracle in itself, and the Den Gang scheme worked well. The children crowded into the tidy-enough garage for their own songs, games and mini-teach and seemed to enjoy the novelty. Then we all worshipped together in the lounge again, overhead projector screen hooked up above the television, and guitar hooked up to the amplifier. Some folk already knew each other—we were to discover before long that Felixstowe is a bit like that—and we just loved each and every one for coming.

Numbers may have been slightly down, but enthusiasm was infectious.

'Yes, we'd love a Wednesday fellowship evening.'

'A Friday morning prayer meeting? Yes, yes . . . no. Not monthly. Weekly would be better.'

'At 7 am? Absolutely!'

So unfolded a pattern for our early days of discovering what God could do. Our twenty-two turned out to be an all-time low, for we climbed gently upwards from then. Graham started playing numbers and dates with God, aiming at a steady increase with irritating accuracy. As for me, I concentrated on guessing how much milk, coffee and tea we would get through, not to mention cakes and biscuits, as that first shared tea set a precedent for an essential preoccupation with food every time we met for anything.

It was good to get to know people and it certainly helped us in the uncomfortable process of settling in a new town and new community. Mind you, sometimes conversations were unnerving. Ever had the feeling that everyone else knows a secret agenda but you?

'So when are you going to build the community centre then?'

Community centre?

'Of course the Church of England will pay for a new building, won't it?'

It will? If only!

'We know what these estates need. It isn't a supermarket and it isn't a church. These estates need small shops and a meeting hall.'

Oh.

'We haven't got any facilities here. Only post-boxes. The young mums have nowhere to go. Nor have the senior citizens. Nowhere for the teenagers. What are you going to do about it?'

Us?

To be fair, we encountered these comments outside our embryonic fellowship, but the expectations were suffocating. The community frustrations were glaringly obvious, but the solutions were not. We seemed to be the target for accumulated disappointments and broken promises dating from the dawn of the estates.

'We've been trying to get something going on these estates ever since they began building ten years ago, but nothing has stuck,' a local Christian informed us. 'There have been many attempts at homegroups, children's work, but all have eventually faltered. You need to know, though, that there has been much prayer for this third of Felixstowe.'

Now that last bit was encouraging. As we struggled to

find a way through the maze of hopes and fears around us, it was very important to uncover a conspiracy of prayer for Cavendish Park that had been quietly reminding the Almighty of the problems and potentials for several years.

Of course we also had the 'You're not going to nick loads of Christians from existing town churches, are you?' comments. And the 'What on earth kind of church meets in a lounge?' Good question! We were in the discovery business ourselves on that one. One of our number had already likened it to worshipping in strawberry yoghurt. Well, we like pink lounges.

If I'm honest, I found it really odd as well. I was used to going to church, for a start. To a place that felt right, and directed my attention to God as I walked in. How could it be the same in our lounge? It was hard to feel very spiritual in the room where I played with the kids, watched telly, sorted photos, even changed nappies sometimes. Squashed cheek by jowl on the unfolded metal chairs we ranged behind the settees, there was somehow no escape, no going through the motions, nowhere to hide.

And when we sang with one guitar and a couple of kids' tambourines, every voice counted. No dreaming in the rafters during the talk either, he who was slipper shod would definitely have noticed. Perhaps those sofas weren't such a good idea after all.

In a big church stashed with pews and people, it can be easy to feel anonymous, can't it? In our lounge that was utterly impossible. So I probably wasn't the only one confronted with the reality or otherwise of what we were doing. I mean, it was pretty daft if it wasn't the truth.

'Is God there for me, can he help me?' The words were little more than a whisper.

It was our first Wednesday fellowship evening.

Through the clatter of mugs, unavoidable eats and chatter afterwards, her voice held a barely suppressed desperation. I recognised the pretty mum with fair hair and large eyes full of questions. She was one of the original thirty-six, contributing herself and two young children to that first surprising Sunday. Tonight those eyes were threatening tears as she asked for hope.

'I know God's there, I've prayed and prayed, but I'm so frightened. It's all been so hard these last few years. I've tried everything and I can't go on any longer.'

Trying to be subtle, which wasn't easy, a friend and I took her to a quieter place, Graham's half-organised study, which was temporary home to all the bits and pieces which hadn't yet decided where they wanted to reside. My friend was Jan, staying with us with her family that week after having had a fire in their house, but that's another story. That first Wednesday I was just glad she was there. The three of us sat down where we could.

'I feel terrible, everything seems to be wrong, my marriage is suffering, I'm so scared.'

Slowly the story of severe post-natal depression came out, hitting hard after the birth of her youngest, a girl.

'My doctor's tried all sorts of tablets, but nothing works. I'm terrified I'm going to lose my sanity and my husband. Can God do anything?'

'What do you want him to do, Lesley?'

'I want to be better. I want this nightmare to stop,' the tears were unchecked now. 'I did enjoy the open-air service, and I feel a sort of warmth here, it feels like God's here. Can he help?'

Well, what could we do? I know I felt overwhelmed by her obvious distress and the complex problems. So when we prayed for her I confess it was one of those oh-goodness-this-is-a-big-one, my-faith-isn't-up-to-this prayers.

You know when you really hope God will give a little chink of light, because you can't see any? Well, she cried, and we felt like it, and we sat together for a while, sharing in the sadness and pain. Then we prayed some more, and her tears gradually subsided. We tried to express our care and she was glad to have unloaded her awesome burden for a while.

I became aware of the continuing hubbub of voices coming from the lounge, and felt duty bound to return. No one was in a hurry to go, which was nice, so it was gone eleven by the time the last coat was found and the last coffee cup washed. Lesley had been calmer when she left, but I was struggling with sadness for her, and doubts. I felt it would be a long time before she would know hope again.

That week the house seemed full of children—well, it was. Our friends had three to add to our two, and none of them was the quiet, retiring type, preferring banister-scaling to book reading. I was getting worried that Paul was taking out moving-house trauma on the Morrises' youngest, as he kept hitting him over the head with a plastic spade. How can children be that violent at only two? We 'growed-ups' were immersed in dreaming up sufficient activities and enough food to prevent total anarchy, frequently sabotaging our own efforts with the fascinating conversations of a friendship long held dear.

'Phone, phone, can someone get it? I'm changing Paul's nappy. Hey, I said—phone!'

Anything to keep clear of a nappy session. I distinguished the ringing from the ridiculous noise in the house, and ran to answer.

'Hallo, who is it?'

'It's Lesley here. I—I just wanted you to know, well, thank you for your prayers. It's so hard to put into words, but though I didn't feel much different last night, I got home and, oh this sounds silly.'

'No Lesley,' I prompted, 'keep going.'

'Well, when I climbed into bed and closed my eyes, all I could see was this picture of Jesus' face, just there. I didn't ask for it to be there, or think of it, it just was. Nothing like that has ever happened to me before. His face was there, with me. And I just feel . . . maybe something has changed.'

We talked for a few minutes. She certainly sounded different. Then, if it is possible to return a phone to its cradle humbly, that's what I did. Lesley had seen more than a chink of light. My awe increased over the next few weeks as Lesley was taken off all her anti-depressants and set free to live again. One, well two, little prayers, and such little faith. Yet a God who graciously met with a daughter of his in need, even in our messy study, bringing healing and life.

I watched as a new awareness of Jesus' presence with her transformed her life, and a bubble of excitement caused a new enthusiasm in me for all the chair-moving, cup-washing, carpet-dirtying and people-meeting of our tiny church's existence.

It changed Lesley's life, and somehow ours too. Suddenly, our little church was in business. For she wasn't the only one. Granted, hers was a wonderfully dramatic and clear-cut example of God using our small set-up, but the strange thing was that other people were meeting God in our lounge too.

'I love it—I feel God is here the moment I walk through the door.'

'This is a special place, I've never known God so close before.'

And I hadn't even hoovered.

Word spread, and friends of friends ventured through our door. I could never quite work out whether it was easier to come to a church-in-a-home because it was less alien than a traditional building or harder because you couldn't escape unnoticed. Still, we tried to make everyone welcome, especially the children.

As for us, we had no option but to willingly open our lives to our new friends. There was no way I could have cleared up the après Sunday afternoon tea debris alone, and soon many volunteers knew my kitchen as well as I did. It's such a good place to talk, isn't it? We all got to know each other over soap suds and tea towels, and it was great. Mucking in together meant we could attempt other events too, like a barbeque in our garden, or rather building site, and a big bonfire party on 5th November.

Then there was the day when I stood looking out of the kitchen window, washing up as usual. For once I was working as slowly as possible, lingering over every spoon. Two grinning faces went past outside, and then back again. Then again. Back and forth they went. I filled the faithful kettle for a cuppa, realising I was almost holding my breath. As I took two steaming cups out through the kitchen door I could see that the workers were almost half way through transforming the dirt ski slope of our garden into a level plateau, and patio to boot. Yes, of course, it was the two muddy men that mattered. Tweedledee and Tweedledum they were nicknamed at that stage, which didn't do justice to their physique at all. One was a policeman who had turned up one day when Graham was gardening in the front (was it the only time?). He said calmly that he had met God at our open-air service and wanted to know what to do to be a Christian. Just like that. The other man was one who had never been to church, and never wanted to go to church,

and didn't want to be a Christian. Yet here he was, shovelling dirt in the vicar's garden, pretending he didn't want to know more. He was Lesley's husband.

So I busied myself in the kitchen, watching them, praying for them. I could almost see God working out there too, encouraging Jerry, melting Rob's antagonism. I was aware again of that bubble of anticipation as slowly Rob allowed himself to trust the church folk and ask about their God.

'I suppose I saw a change in my wife that was, to me, unexplainable,' he was later to say. 'She and I were at an all-time low before this, and then suddenly it started to improve. I began to wonder what this church business was all about, until in the end I felt I had to find out for myself.'

Rob graduated from the garden to the lounge. We had

28

a new, wonderful garden, and he discovered a new, wonderful God. I breathed again as two new members were added safely to the family of God.

Perhaps it was going to be OK here after all. Perhaps it would all come together.

Perhaps.

2

Worship and Warts

The hammering on the door went on and on. One of those times when you try to ignore something, but it just keeps on pestering.

Bang, bang, bang! I pulled the bedcovers round my ears and tried to get back into my dream—such a nice one, we were on holiday and the sun was shining and—

'Yikes, it's Friday. Get up! It's them!'

Graham shot out of bed, sending the duvet flying. I've never seen him move so fast. I opened my mouth to protest at the draught when realisation dawned.

'It's Friday! We've overslept! It's prayers!'

We stumbled downstairs, dressing-gowned and bleary, to discover the faithful Friday seven o'clockers laughing on the doorstep. Great. Still, it hadn't happened before, we'd managed to stagger down in good time up till now, and I was sure Graham was too cross with himself for it to happen again. So we collapsed on the sofas in the lounge as usual and began our hour of prayer together, fighting the temptation to drift off again. I felt ashamed.

The other six people had had to travel to be here and I hadn't even managed the stairs properly. But somehow this ridiculous hour—Graham and I never were 'morning' people—held a special quietness and strength. Some who came had hardly ever prayed before, and it was lovely to see them gaining confidence in talking to God. Graham was reading from Psalm 145: 'The Lord is gracious and compassionate, slow to anger and rich in love. The Lord is good to all; he has compassion on all he has made.'

The familiar words dropped into our companionable silence and caught a fresh relevance as I realised that to others they were totally new. I was infected by the sense of eagerness to learn more about this God who was becoming real. I too came at well-worn truths with a questioning mind and growing excitement. So what about prayer? How do we pray? What is it for? How do we respond to God?

31

Crash!

The children. They were awake. Should I leave them to it, stay here with my new-found friends and their new-found God and—

Thump, bang.

I gave in. I really had hoped they'd sleep on for once. I dragged myself out of the sofa and crept out, torn between people, wanting to be in two places at once, glad and grateful that I had the chance to join in the prayers at all, yet frustrated because the house was still our home and had to function as such.

'Mum! Paul's broken my hairband!'

They do keep your feet on the ground, don't they, children? The trouble was, I didn't always want them there— my feet, that is.

'Mum, Mum! Stop him, he's got my puzzles out. And he smells, Mum. Shall I help you change his nappy?'

Why do little children make me feel so unspiritual? A moment ago my enthusiasm for godly things knew no bounds, yet now resentment clouded my view as I resigned myself to clearing up the mess my offspring had created within two minutes of waking up.

'Paul, give me those puzzles. No, not like that, the other way up. No!'

Aargh! Pieces of Noddy littered the floor. Oops! We mustn't shout too loud with a lounge full of happy holy people.

'Come on Paul, let's de-smell you. Judy, put on your dressing gown, and you can go and sit on Daddy's lap if you're quiet.'

'Can I, can I?' sang my five year old, bumpily rushing downstairs.

When I peeped through the windowed lounge doors a few minutes later, Paul a more respectable bundle of boy cuddled in my arms, Judy was curled happily on Graham's lap, carefully watching everybody. Aware that she was hugely enjoying being included in the 'grown-up' prayer time, my emotions did another about-turn. It was good that the children were part of it all. It was good that they saw faith in action.

I dumped Paul on the kitchen floor with some toys—his—and picked up our well-used kettle, mentally counting how many there would be to squash round our dining-room table for breakfast. Did it matter if they heard me shouting at the kids, I wondered, grabbing cereal packets and bowls. It was so much nicer to pretend that I never did and that our family life was sweetness and light most of the time. That I coped easily with two demanding little people, housework, washing, cooking, cleaning, ferrying to school, mother and toddlers, packing lunches, preparing for the regular transformations into 'church', that I sailed gaily through it.

But when my home was also a church, and the door always open, where could I hide? When indeed I wanted to open my heart to these precious God-searching folk, I had to accept they would see me, warts and all. I didn't want that bit. I wanted them to think me nicer than I am.

'Hallo, is the kettle boiled yet?' A friendly voice broke through my reverie, and I realised the prayers were done.

'Yep, it's ready and so is the toast I think,' I replied, smiling in response. Doubts driven aside by the chance to chat and eat together, I asked Lesley to collect the drinks orders.

'Hi love, what's the smell?' Hubby poked his head into the kitchen.

'Smell? What smell—oh no! The toast! I've burnt it again!'

Warts and all.

Yet it was all any of us had to give, building a church from scratch. We had only ourselves, and Graham had determined from the start that there would be reality in our worship and life together. No outward show, no form of religion if it wasn't reflecting what was happening on the inside between each of us and God. It seemed that God was happy with that too, certainly from my experience.

It also seemed to be working. Quietly yet steadily, more people were joining us. Some, of course, just popped in for the odd couple of services to see what Graham and his Mickey Mouse church—yes, we'd heard it said—were like. It seemed ironic that others didn't count us as a 'real' church when we were striving so hard for reality ourselves. We wanted good relationships with the other town churches, and were extremely aware that our few mature Christian families had been released from these churches to join us. Our housing estate was indeed at one end of an old-established parish. With only three parishes covering the whole of Felixstowe, we needed their goodwill. We had tried not to test this too severely, by beginning with our shared tea and family service afternoons, but soon felt that a once-a-month morning service would be appropriate, and also enable us to have an adult evening service.

'The body of Christ, broken for you.'

Our first evening communion was really memorable. I was surprised again by how unavoidable the Lord's presence seemed, even in our lounge, and in spite of the rush to get the children to bed, and the room ready on time. It was almost as if the very air became saturated with God, and the bread and wine very precious as we passed it from one to another with the powerful words.

'The blood of Christ, shed for you.'

No robes or altar rail, nor even smart suits and well-tried formula, just a group of people, some words from the Anglican Service Book (ASB) and requested songs helping us to quieten our minds and focus on God. So different, yet so familiar. God meeting us because we desired to meet him.

'I think we'll have a congregational meeting,' Hubby announced after the service. It was often fun creating *ex nihilo*. 'All the best church-planting courses tell you that it takes a team to do it. Now we know why it's so exhausting—it's just us. So let's get everyone together and make one.'

It was the beginning of the school autumn term. We'd survived our first couple of months amazingly well, though it felt like a couple of years since that open-air service. Now we all—twenty adults in all—gathered to discuss the future.

'This is not my church,' began Graham, 'it belongs to all of us. It depends on each one of us, and we are all members of the team.'

It was true that we all noticed who was there each time, which was only natural with total numbers around the thirties.

'So what do you think? What are your ideas for our church's life and growth?'

'I like the prayer meetings,' volunteered Joan. 'Let's keep them going.'

'OK. We'll try and get up for them!' responded Graham.

'I'm enjoying our fellowship evenings,' added Lesley, 'but I feel I know so little. Can we do something about the basics of Christianity?'

'Yeah, I'd like that too.'

'Me too.'

So that seemed to be a good idea.

We called the course 'Square One', Graham basing its

six-week content on a similar home-grown project run at our previous church. It was back to the familiar can-I-get-the-kids-to-bed-by-7.45-and-have-the-downstairs-ready fight for me, but mostly I made it—just. I felt a real hypocrite sometimes for growling at our precious offspring seconds before presenting a smiling face at the door. Am I the only one who does this? I just didn't seem able to get things organised far enough in advance to avoid it. So it was often with a strong sense of my own inadequacy that I joined the dozen or so adults in our well-used lounge. Yet as the evening progressed, every time I became caught up in an exhilarating sense of discovery and excitement, as together we explored the world's best-selling book. We hammered through doubts and questions, starting right at the beginning with Adam and Eve's fateful choice. We created for each other a 'safe' place to express feelings and fears and challenged each other to test the truth of what we were reading.

Square One was to be repeated many times, but that first run was a special one as we all got to know each other better. Every week there were stories to report of relationships with God coming alive. Take Joan for instance. One Tuesday night she was fairly squeaking with excitement.

'You know, when Graham invited us to attend this course, I wasn't sure I should be here as I've been going to church for most of my life. I mean, I was confirmed at thirteen, and I know stained-glass windows very well, and this church hasn't got any. Talking of that, it hasn't got much else I've been used to either.'

We would have asked her more about the differences at this point, but no one could get a word in edgeways, she was so lit up.

'Anyway, as I did decide to do the course, I thought I ought to make the most of it and do some homework on the Old Testament. I don't know it very well. Can you believe it? I chose Leviticus to start with. I suppose I thought that if I understood the laws of the Jews, then the rest of the Bible's customs and background would be easier to grasp. Have you read it? It's rather boring, all repeats, but I stuck with it, every verse of it. I even began to wake up at three o'clock in the mornings to read it. Then I hit the bit about the way different animals, always young unblemished males, were offered as sacrifices to take away people's sins. And early Sunday morning, and I mean early, I suddenly saw Jesus as the young perfect male being sacrificed on the cross for me, my sins. It was so overwhelming I felt myself saying, 'No Lord, no, not just for me, I'm not worthy of you.' It was so vivid, I can't get over it. It's like Jesus suddenly walked right out of the book, no longer just an historical figure, but here, alive,

37

here with me now by my side. I'm sure there should be a hole in my Bible now, where he came out. He is my best mate, he's always with me. Isn't it amazing?'

Sparkling eyes and a huge smile confirmed Joan's words. We were all pleased for her, and through Leviticus, of all books!

Another evening I will always remember was later on, when we were talking about the Holy Spirit.

'As you have read, God's Holy Spirit gives all sorts of gifts to us,' explained Graham. 'Some of these are things like administration or giving, some appear more supernatural, like gifts of healing, but they are all given for the common good, for us to give away if you like.'

'What's this speaking in tongues, Graham?'

'Well, Jerry, that's like a special prayer language the Spirit gives for us to use to praise God and for when we run out of English.'

'Sounds good. I'll go for that!'

'Yes, but hasn't there been a lot of conflict about it?' said a voice whose owner was more familiar with church life.

Jerry's face registered his surprise.

'Conflict?! How could there be conflict over something so wonderful?'

Aah, the refreshing approach of new Christians! It was such a breath of fresh air. Jerry to the rescue again. It wasn't the only time, either, that Jerry with his wonderfully straightforward approach to the things of God, got us out of a hole. He would often wander round for a cuppa to 'talk God' and one afternoon happened upon Graham plonked on the floor in the dining room, surrounded by piles of money.

'Having fun there, Graham?'

Groan.

'Just sorting out the finances, Jerry. We're such a young

church, but there seems to be so much to look after already.'

'Would you like me to do the money for you?'

Just like that. Well, if you can't trust a policeman, you're a bit stuck aren't you?

'Thanks, Jerry, that'd be great.' Relief and gratitude were obvious. 'Another cuppa mate?'

So Jerry became our treasurer, from the start attacking the task with a light-hearted God-will-provide approach which belied the hard work he put in over many hours. For example, I remember the day he appeared on the doorstep a few months later with the news that we had only seventeen pence left in the church accounts.

'Is there anything you want me to buy, Graham? A stamp perhaps?'

But he was not in the least bit worried, and God seemed constantly to validate his trust that the money would come in when we needed it, and none of us knew in those early days quite what a job he was letting himself in for.

Neither, I suspect, did others who volunteered to *do* as well as come to the fledgling congregation. With more children coming, Graham needed some serious help for the Den Gang, especially as the plan was to reverse the process and keep the children in for the beginning of the service and then let them have some time just for them afterwards. The kitchen was employed for one age group, the crèche was in the hastily-cleared dining room, and the faithful garage now had a heater in it. So a Den Gang team was formed, headed by Gill, a gifted and gracious Christian lady whose passion was working with children. Another mature couple, Ivan and Ann, were pressed into service, forming a worship team with Graham, so that he and his slippers shared the leading of worship and preaching.

'I can't believe we've only been in action for four months,' I declared to anyone who would listen one Sunday, after our monthly evening service. As usual, no one wanted to leave and I was considering offering yet another round of tea and coffee. Maybe it had taken us all by surprise, this vibrant sense of God being there when we met together, and I suppose I never wanted to move from its warmth either.

'It hardly seems possible that we've done so much, from just the four of us to all of you. Regular Sunday services and weekly meetings.'

'Don't forget our Friday morning prayers.' I think it was Rob.

'As if I would! No seriously, there's been that joint Harvest service we had with the parish church and Baptists, and the Hallelujah party we did for the kids at Hallowe'en.'

'*And* we've had our first baptism service,' piped up Gill.

'Yep, that was a good day,' put in Graham, 'especially as it was church census day. Our numbers looked really impressive with all those visiting relatives.'

'Talking of numbers, I was really pleased how many came to the Tearcraft open day too,' I added. The dining room had taken a break from shared food and sticky crèche fingers, and been transformed into a third-world bazaar, as we'd taken the plunge and ordered beautifully hand-crafted products from developing countries across the globe to sell. Tearcraft, the trading arm of the charity Tear Fund, which we'd started to support as a church in October, imported these goods from responsibly and fairly run producer groups. With some shops and volunteer reps like us selling the wares, these craftspeople received a proper price for their hard work and a

Christian input too. We were impressed by the Tearcraft commitment to dignity and hope for people who did not have them, and it was satisfying and fun to see how well the goods had sold. It seemed important to be giving as well, thinking of others, not just ourselves and creating a positive precedent for the future.

We were also aware of being supported ourselves. Slipper man's salary was paid by the Church of England, the diocese had bought our house, and the deanery (local Anglican churches) insisted on paying Graham's working expenses and various setting-up costs. It was wonderful to be free of initial financial worries, and to know we were believed in. It meant a great deal. So we wanted to give what we could, even though we were so dependent on others.

The hammering on the door went on and on. Now it was the bell. We've been here before. But no, this time it really was the middle of the night. Always the first to wake—I guess that's what babies do for you—I decided that discretion was the greater part of valour and poked Graham. Hard.

'I'm not going, it's two o'clock. Definitely your turn.'

Hubby did his pretending-to-be-awake act and put his dressing gown on inside out. Once downstairs, I heard the door click open and a woman's voice loudly request use of our phone. Suspicious, Graham asked why. She wanted to call a taxi. Graham was obviously worried and invited her in.

At this point I decided I had better eavesdrop properly, so rolled out of bed and crept to the top of the stairs. The lady seemed distressed but mainly desirous of using our phone, I could tell that. Hubby was clearly not awake properly as he kept asking solicitous questions, and out tumbled a garbled story of boyfriends, shotguns and lack of money, adopting a religious flavour when she discovered he was a minister. Let her use the phone, Graham. I'm all for this open-house business, but there are limits. Just when I thought I would have to intervene and stop him offering her a lift home, he came to his senses and showed her the phone. I really do want to be welcoming to everyone, Lord, but it's two o'clock in the morning. The taxi arrived and its driver bundled our visitor into the back.

'We'll take her, that's all right. Oh yes, we know her. Does this all the time. Don't worry about it. 'Night now.'

Of course it took us ages to get to sleep after that. Paul woke up later on anyway. I lay there wondering. Our night-time caller had been so unexpected, so unnerving somehow, one of so many surprises in this new life to which we had been called. It was hard to know how to respond sometimes. It had been such a graphic demonstration of the fact that we never knew who or what was going to land on our doorstep next. I wanted to be ready to respond to all in the way God would have me. I was excited about what God was doing. About our worship together.

But I wanted to hide the warts.

3

Cracked!

It was that time again.

Perhaps we should give up Sunday lunch. It was not very digestible anyhow, on top of irrepressibly mounting adrenalin, and it would save on washing-up. That would be one less job to get done before 4.30 in the afternoon. It was amazing how long it took to turn our modest four-bedroom house into a church.

Every week it was metamorphosis. The table had to be turned round, boxes of crèche toys readied, chairs moved into the lounge and study, and double doors opened between the two rooms. Then the sofas must be rearranged, OHP installed, guitar tuned, and sermon lost and found. Finally the kitchen needed to be cleared and cups put out. It seemed to go on for ever and we were always only just ready when the doorbell began to ring.

Then the same needed doing in reverse afterwards and various mini-versions throughout the week. Yet still the wonder of what was happening gripped and inspired me even as we prepared our home for another invasion. It still surprised me that week after week folk would pile in through our front door. I was still holding my breath, so to speak, waiting for the bubble to burst. It all felt so fragile and delicate. There was one couple with a very young baby, Pollyanna, and her newly-expressed hold on life seemed to mirror that of the church. There we were, with no guarantee of a future, yet glad to be alive. It was a beginning. And inevitably, just as a baby takes more than you thought possible to give (well, ours did), so our tiny church community took over our lives completely too.

'Graham—phone.'

'Di, can you get the door, I'm just talking to someone.'

'But Mum! I want my dolls in the lounge, I don't want to move them.'

'Graham, I forgot the milk for this evening. The kids are in the bath—can you take over and I'll pop out and get some?'

'Fred is in a fix again, I'll have to go and see him. I know I said I'd stay in but. . . .'

'Graham—phone.'

It was always the phone! It was always a challenge: the distraught daughter at the other end whose mother had just died; the young mum who had heard that a new vicar was here and wondered whether we 'did' (baptised) babies, because the chap in her area wouldn't; the church friend upset because his wife could not understand his new-found faith.

Actually, the breaking-point was the carpet. That carpet, gloriously new and unlike anything we had had before. For a start, we had chosen it. You couldn't feel the concrete underneath because it was real pile, not industrial. You could almost—though not quite—sink your toes into it. But it was plain and pale pink. I think, looking back, that parents on both sides tried to tell us. It may have been the headiness of choosing for ourselves, but we did not listen. It was agony watching it lose its glory. Shoes after shoes after shoes trampled it. We tried that awful transparent plastic covering in the hall, but it wouldn't stay where it was put and crawled halfway up the wall. We tried an oversize coir mat by the door to scrape up the dirt. We wished we could ask everyone to take off their shoes, but we couldn't. It was no use. They came, they trampled, and our carpet began to die. It shouldn't have mattered of course. What was a clean, fresh carpet compared to the unexpected joys of lives changed and a church born?

I suppose the problem was that I couldn't keep up with it. I just couldn't keep up with the cleaning. It was enough of an effort getting tidy each time a meeting rolled round, and that was only ever downstairs. We had quickly decided that our open-house policy had to exclude upstairs, or there would have been nowhere to hide the rubble. There always seemed to be the next event, and the next. It was all so surprising, the way people came, relaxed and responded to God that I did not realise how I was struggling to keep up with my side of it all. It just seemed that everywhere I went, all the houses were spotless, neat, organised and peaceful, while I felt involved in a perpetual battle to hold back total chaos. Our ever-open door meant I was now risking exposure. Other people managed this housework thing, why couldn't I? I began to feel that I must look to others how my carpet looked to me. Imperfect, stained, in need of improvement.

Yet there was no time to indulge in too much self-deprecation. It nagged underneath, but was consistently overlaid by the small, but precious miracles around. There were new relationships with God, new friendships and new hope. It was worth the escalating demands on our house, time, energies, and even carpet. It was worth all those edges beginning to feel frayed.

Yet the whole process also threw up questions as well. Why didn't God do this for everyone? Why were some people open to him and others not? Why this person and not that one? And OK, I admit it. Why my teeth?

Teeth? Well, it all started before we ever arrived in Felixstowe, but boy, did it explode after we had. In case exploding teeth sound a bit frightful, let me explain. The story began in Nottingham, some five years previously. It went something like this:

Me   Dentist, I've noticed my front teeth are moving apart. They are starting to stick out a bit. I want a brace.

Dentist   OK, let's see what we can do. I'll take out this tooth here to make some room. . . .'

Me   Ouch!

Dentist   And this one here as well. Oh dear, it's pulled the one out behind it as well. Oh dear, the holding bone seems to have snapped too. It's coming out as well. Don't move, I'll have to stitch you up.

Me   !!!

Dentist   This hasn't happened to me before. Hang on.

Me   Gurgle. (Meaning, your hands are shaking.)

Dentist   Nearly there. I'm sorry, I don't know why. You will have to be careful of infection.

Me   Oh.

Dentist   Done I think. You will need a lift home.

Bed! I just wanted to get to bed and sleep and pretend nothing had happened. To say I was in a state of shock would be an understatement.

The forces rallied. Mum arrived. I cancelled everything

I'VE NEVER SEEN A CASE QUITE LIKE YOURS...

except my six-week-old baby, and tried to recover. But I was badly frightened, even though the threatened infection never materialised. Fear set in and I did not darken the door of a dentist for a long time.

It was over four years later before I screwed up enough courage to have another go. By this time the gap between my two front teeth was very noticeable. We had moved to Ipswich by that time, so it was to a different dentist I went. He didn't have fangs or two horns sticking out of his head, so I tried to tell myself to be calm as he poked about in my mouth. My stomach was churning though, with the butterflies doing overtime. Are dentists human? They have such power, certainly over me. Yet this one seemed open to the brace idea, but wanted a second opinion.

So next it was off to the local hospital, another place I dread. X-rays and white-coated, official-faced medics towered over me. Then it was verdict time.

'Mrs Archer, it seems you have a problem here. Your teeth have moved because you have a disease in the holding bone. This bone is slowly disintegrating and eventually you will lose all your teeth. There is nothing we can do.'

Did they try and tell me gently? I don't know. The facts were stark anyway. Senses reeled as Hubby steered me down the polished corridors towards the cafeteria. No! No! No! screamed inside me. Nightmare. It cannot be. Terror. But I'm so healthy. But I don't even eat sweets, well, not many. But I try so hard to eat and live right. But this is not fair.

I cupped shaking hands round my mug of tea. What should I think? How was I to cope with the fear? But . . . but God? What about God, the God who had always been there for me, seeing me through so many ups and downs? Surely he would intervene, surely he would give me hope. Surely he could change this dreadful situation, though no one else could?

With the desperation of the drowning, I clung to that thought. He had healed others, would he not heal me?

That weekend, still ravaged with shock, I could not get to church fast enough. It just happened to be a service for healing on the Sunday evening. Nothing would have kept me from asking for prayer. Self-consciousness, shyness, doubts—all were thrown to the wind—and as some dear friends prayed for me I felt a rush of warmth through my body, an overwhelming sense of God's presence. For the first time since I had heard the condemning prognosis, my mind quieted, and the petrified whirling slowed. God did care for me. It was going to be OK.

I returned home that evening a good deal calmer and more hopeful. Healing had been asked for, healing would come. I inspected my teeth in the mirror to see if anything

48

had happened yet. No. Oh well. Perhaps it would happen overnight.

Even before I opened my eyes the next morning, I was running my tongue over my teeth, feeling for a difference. There was nothing yet, but perhaps God would do it gradually. I knew he could do it. I even shared my conviction with a few friends, just to make sure. Day followed day, and there was nothing. Not yet, not yet. It was weeks now, surely it was going to happen soon. A month, two months, surely now? But surely the question mark materialised at the end of my prayers. I kept on believing, I kept on asking for healing prayer but the question mark intensified, thickened, and began to dominate. I kept on hoping but it was too late. The battle had begun.

By the time we landed in Felixstowe, it had become something I did not want to think about, because I was losing. The calm trust I had received seemed to have evaporated, and panic-ridden, mind-numbing fear was beginning its rampant ride through my soul. As those first precious days of our fledgling church unfolded, I employed every denial tactic I knew to stop myself from dwelling on the subject. How could God be so close and yet so far, all at once? This was spoiling everything, nagging underneath, trying to invalidate the new adventures of faith to which we had been called.

'I think you should go back to the dentist. Let's just see what he says.'

I knew I should too. But I did not want to hear it. I snapped back at Graham—not for the last time. He felt helpless to aid me, I was so well locked inside my fears. Any suggestion generally received the same treatment. It is a wonder he still has a head.

I found it so hard to face the facts. Healing had not happened—yet? My teeth were not looking any better. I tried not to admit it, but the front ones were even starting to feel wobbly and loose.

In the end, I had to go.

I had no guts to do it alone, and dragged Hubby and son along with me. Or did they drag me? How I got myself in that chair I do not know.

'Well, Mrs Archer, the disease seems to have progressed somewhat. Clearly a brace is out of the question as the bone is not strong enough. With the condition of your teeth, all I can suggest for the front two is that you have them out and replace them with dentures.'

That did it. Now I really was expecting the forked tail.

'And, and what if I don't, how long will I keep my teeth?'

'It's hard to say—depends on the progression—anything from now to ten years. Meanwhile you need a filling at the back there.'

A filling! What was the point?

'Think about my suggestion. Let me know.'

Dentures? Never. I wanted my own teeth, and I wanted them better. I did not want what was happening. It is impossible to describe adequately my state of mind at this point. I was angry, yes, and desperate, and terribly afraid. I felt as if I was being rushed on an express train over the edge of an abyss. I had no control. God had no control, there was none. Heaven was silent, yet the voice of reason served only to rebuke that this was such a relatively little thing to bear. It didn't make any difference.

I was not going to go near a dentist, ever again.

All this internal pressure had to go somewhere. I could not hide it from my new friends for ever. So it was that Sunday evening services in our house found me often in a miserable heap about the whole affair. Here I was, testifying to others about a God who is real, yet having to confess that he had hit a situation with me that he did not seem able to cope with. I could not stop the tears, frequently, any more than I could halt the fears. Joan would cuddle me in the kitchen, supporting and encouraging. Lesley wanted to help. Dave prayed for me, encouraged me. They were so kind. Alison said, 'Don't you see, it's all right? We don't know the answer either, but we are so glad you haven't got it all together. Can't you see you are encouraging us to drop our masks, to be ourselves, to own up to the things we struggle with?'

In a funny way that was a bit comforting. It was an unbelievably painful way to encourage reality and honesty among us. I felt so full of fear and failure. Yet it was right that this was one huge wart that I could not hide upstairs. It did hurt though, and I hated the accompanying sense of isolation when the bridges my friends built towards me never quite reached. It wasn't their fault, it was mine.

Graham too was sensing his own time of isolation. Not only did he have a stumbling wife to contend with, but also the unsettling dynamic of being on the edge of the Church of England that he worked for. What we were doing and the way we were doing it felt very much out of the mainstream and earned a few askance looks. We had been asked to 'keep the window open for ecumenical co-operation', which was fine, but it left Graham with the challenge of creating an identity for the church, with no pattern to follow. For a while we had a reference group comprised of local Christians and people with wider ecumenical experience to help us reflect on the ethos of the church. But we were breaking new ground, and it felt very much trial and error.

* * *

'We wish you a merry Christmas,
We wish you a merry Christmas. . . .'

It was hard to believe we had been here for five months already. They had been ridiculously full. Sometimes it seemed like five years. Yet that first Christmas was such a special time. Warts, traumas and pains were forgotten as we celebrated in style. We all squashed in the church— our lounge, study, corridor and dining room—for a Christmas meal. Tables were squeezed into impossible spaces, with boxes doubling as chairs, and decorations over everything. There was no room for elbows but it was a precious opportunity for this new family of God to enjoy traditional fare together for the first time.

Then we took over the local school for a special praise service, inviting everyone we knew. Next it was out on the streets, Tweedledee and Tweedledum leading the way as we terrorised the estates with our carol singing. The tape and amplifier bumped along in the pram, home-made lanterns assisted with intermittent enthusiasm, and voices sang ancient words with recently-discovered meaning. We offered mince pies to all we met, most of whom could not believe we did not want money. It all culminated in a Christmas Eve crib service for all in our lounge, and a midnight communion in the warm glow of a myriad candles (the Health and Safety people would not have approved). The whole season was shot through with the infectious excitement of so many celebrating this event properly for the first time. Not only was a new church family enjoying its first Christmas, but there were constant reminders of what the miracle of God being born man meant in real terms for us today.

'This time last year—I cannot believe it—I'd never have thought I'd be doing this, singing round the streets and enjoying it.'

'It's amazing, Christmas means something at last, after all these years of food and booze!'

'I still can't take in how wonderful Christmas is, to think God came as a baby for me, and now I know him.'

It was just the best time, and helped to put life back into perspective for a somewhat travel-weary Christian like me. Perhaps this bit of the journey was worth while after all, whatever it was costing, and one day Joan hesitated on our doorstep before rushing off.

'I know you feel bad about it,' she ventured, 'but it helps me that you struggle with things. I just would not relate to you if you could do everything, if you had all the answers. So please don't mind.'

No, it did not make me feel better about myself. It did not make the battle any easier, but it did make me see that others did not mind me being me.

Perhaps I had to learn to live with the warts, rather than cry for a cure.

4

Growing Pains

A brand-new year ahead. For many of us, not like any New Year we had faced before. New challenges, new friends, new allegiances. A new relationship with God.

A general buzz of excitement helped to counteract the sense of risk as we wondered what the new year would hold, whether God would continue to bring people, and whether we would rise to the challenge.

'It must be very rewarding and thrilling.' I had joined one of my Ipswich friends for coffee. 'It is wonderful that you have so many people already.'

'I guess thirty-five is an improvement on four,' I grinned, 'and I don't want to underestimate that. But I can't believe what hard work it is, and how drained I feel after such a great Christmas.'

It often puzzled me, this caring for people bit, and really going for stuff you believe in. Why was it so exhausting? When so much was going so well? It was still tempting to wish I was a super Christian, the sort in books, who seem to relish in the struggles, conquer the obstacles every time, have a fantastic unshakeable faith, and just love going to the dentist. Yet here I was, a fallible, wavering specimen! Added to the toll of these first, amazing, overwhelming months of Cavendish Community Church there were two bereavements in our extended families, and I really needed to hear an encouraging testimony at our New Year service. It was Tweedledum, I mean Jerry, our treasurer.

I met God through the open-air service on the green. I went along, saw Graham, but felt that he would be far too busy to speak to me. I saw him again in his front garden, spoke to him and he gave me a CCC information sheet. I know God a lot better now.

I have gained so much by knowing God. I believe I am more calm, though my wife may disagree! I have the joy of fellowship. I have made wonderful friends over the last four months. I really look forward to the Square One meetings that we have on Tuesday evenings, so much so that for the first time in my life I say at work that I have to go home. I am a workaholic but for this—I really look forward to leaving to learn more about God. When I read the Bible I look at each word intensely, wanting to know more about it. I have gained an awful lot from devotional readings with daily Bible study notes. I pray for guidance. In the last four months I have gone to the Bible three times for help. Very difficult problems at work are sorted out with help from the Bible.

Since becoming a Christian I get hurt when people blaspheme. I also get hurt when I hear different people like missionaries come to fellowship meetings to tell us about their experiences. It makes me realise how lucky I am for being well fed and warm. That hurts as well. I am learning to pray about that so that I can do something in a more practical way.

I have a long way to go in 1990. I don't know if testimonies talk about the future, but for me I want to learn so that I can get confirmed over the next year.

I will finish with faith. Faith is being certain of something
that you cannot see.

Faith for the new year. That was what we needed. So the
scene was set for the next step. Or so we thought.

It was, as usual, the phone. That impartial harbinger of
good news and bad. This time it was the latter.

'Graham, remember me? We worked together on the
music for that joint harvest service last year.'

'Oh yes, hallo Andrew.'

'Can I come and see you? My wife and I—we have left
our church. I think our fellowship has just blown up.'

'What?!'

'Our pastor has been promoting some far-reaching
prophecies which we feel are unbiblical and dangerous.
We've left. Can we join you?'

They were just the first. Memories of the pain involved
forbid me to divulge more of the details, but suffice it to
say that there were enough members of this particular
local house church who were sufficiently unhappy to
leave, for it to collapse. Most house churches are terrific,
and we value their leaders among our spiritual teachers.
Sadly, this one was not. In fact, it felt a bit like the domino
effect, as one after another they left, and not a few found
their way to CCC's door. Bewilderment, pain and anger
were evident, as we attempted to demonstrate appropriate care. Whatever the rights and wrongs of the situation
in God's eyes, the people who joined us felt a great sense
of betrayal, that most devastating of human emotions.

We were also faced with a practical problem.

'Graham, I've finally run out of mugs. I've used everything—how many people are here today?'

Hubby quietly squeezed his way through for a head
count.

'No wonder you've run out. We have sixty-seven people in this house, and yes I've included the ones sitting up the stairs and hanging out the windows.'

'What are we going to do?'

'Find another venue.'

The hunt was on. A local school on our patch was a possibility but the rent was too high. Fortunately, we had already arranged for the following Sunday service to be held in St Philip's, the daughter church in our parish, which was in the middle of the neighbouring estate. We borrowed it for Pollyanna's dedication, as we had known numbers would be swollen for that. The church and she were entering a new phase of life. The six months, marked by the New Year, seemed to mark an increasing hold on life for both the baby girl and our baby church. But back to the quest. In the middle of starting another Square One course, beginning a new series of fellowship evenings, and initiating a daytime homegroup for ladies—with accompanying children where necessary—we were trying to find a new home fast. In the end it was not far away.

Just up the road was a communal lounge for the residents of the surrounding bungalows, the Reynolds Court Housing Association complex.

The news was that we could use it for Sunday services if all the residents agreed. They did! So the beginning of February saw us trekking the four hundred metres up the road, loaded with chairs, milk, amplifiers, PA, OHP screen, boxes, children's material . . . the list went on and on. It was a ridiculously mammoth upheaval, and we were eventually to invest in a small box trailer to assist with our nomadic existence, but it was worth it. The lounge was large enough for seventy, there was a big kitchen, and room to expand again. Some of the residents came to join us, and we used two of their bungalows as substitute garages for the Den Gangs to meet in.

Suddenly we were going out to church again. Graham had to shed his slippers and find his shoes. I had to admit it was something of a relief to have the main church meeting out of our house, and for the era of total domestic reorganisation to be over. Yet I was glad we still held other meetings and services in our strawberry-yoghurt lounge, and I think others were too.

'I know we have to move, but it does seem strange. I'm so fond of your lounge, so much has happened for me there. Reynolds Court just doesn't seem the same.' This from Joan.

'It is going to take a while to get used to worshipping there. It is all so new and different.' Lesley I think.

'But we can breathe again, grow again.' I retorted. 'The church is the people not the building.' I had learnt that lesson well, if nothing else.

'Yes, but your house is where we met God for the first time, where we learnt to worship.'

Well, I guess that will just have to go down as a mystery to me. Or perhaps the grace of God. Anyhow, it was exciting that we had had to move because the numbers necessitated it. That was undeniably good.

But it was a challenge as well. A challenge to settle down in a new place, and a challenge to settle down together. For the demise of the house church turned out to be a blessing for us as many special folk joined CCC, but the process of getting to know each other and becoming a unified body was rather akin to two fast-flowing streams at their meeting point. Turbulence, froth, eddies and swirls ensued as the pain of what the newcomers had been through met the new-found faith and struggling existence of those there from earlier days. However, it was not long

before a new corporate identity emerged, a richer fuller current flowing onwards. Richer because of the people themselves, and also the gifts they brought with them. It has to be said that our music was greatly enhanced at this point. Our quota of wires suddenly quadrupled, as Andrew set up his keyboard and Graham's guitar was no longer the sole accompaniment to our songs. Rob was inspired to learn the guitar too, and the embryo of a worship band was there. We became bolder in exploring new songs and Graham was able to begin sharing the worship leading as well as the preaching.

It was at this point that we also took the plunge and initiated morning services, by common consent. Once a month we kept to the original pattern of shared tea and family service, but otherwise we felt it was time to create the morning slot. At the same time, building up good relationships with the other churches in town remained a priority, especially the nearest ones, our parish church and the local Baptist and Methodist. We knew we had really made it when first the archdeacon and then the bishop came to visit.

Our first Easter saw us joining with most of the other town churches for a Good Friday service in the middle of the town, having created our own pattern for the previous week and the Sunday, complete with hot-cross buns. Like the thrill of our first Christmas together, this was again a festival which many had not celebrated in any other way than chocolate before. But then without the Easter story we would not be here at all:

Why is Easter special to me?

Well, on Good Friday as long ago as 1959 when I was fifteen, there was a programme on the television that I watched about what it meant for Jesus to die on the cross for me. That programme stayed in my mind over the next year. I knew what I should do. I should ask Jesus to come and live in my heart. But somehow I didn't. However, I kept thinking about it.

My grandmother was a Christian, and by the time Easter 1960 came around, she had decided it was time to help things along, so she arranged to take me on a youth event on Good Friday evening. The youth I met there invited me to go on a ramble with them on Easter Monday. On the Sunday I found myself at the back of the church singing the chorus: 'He lives, he lives, Christ Jesus lives today. You ask me how I know he lives? He lives within my heart.' Only I knew that he didn't live in my heart. The next day was the ramble. Afterwards, I stood in the church hall watching some of them play football and I knew why they were different to me. So as I stood there I invited Jesus into my life as Saviour, and I knew something had happened.

I was a Christian. I had some good years and not so good ones after that. I grew up, got married and had my first child.

Things were not always easy and I longed for a deeper relationship with Jesus. Then one day the Lord spoke to me just before another Easter and said that things would be different after it. Just after Easter I joined a ladies' group for prayer and Bible study. I learned from them about being baptised with the Holy Spirit, and about all the charismatic gifts. Two of the ladies prayed for me to receive God's Holy Spirit, full to overflowing. At first I thought nothing had happened, but then I began to pray in a strange language, for what I thought was a few minutes. I was told afterwards that as I began to pray someone saw a picture of a dove and a flagon of oil over my head; and that I prayed for four-and-a-half hours!

After that I was like a different person. All the loneliness and emptiness inside disappeared. My husband said I was different and six weeks later he too received the baptism of the Holy Spirit.

These are not the only times the Lord has touched my life, but they marked the big changes and they are why Easter is special to me.

Thank you Janet. She and her husband David were two we did speak to on that first open-air service, and we have enjoyed their fellowship ever since.

And talking of fellowship, Graham and I once went on a holiday where an optional 'jeep safari' was offered as a day trip. Staring at the advertising poster, the cluster of holiday-makers around us decided that they could not take the risk. After all, one never knew whom one was going to be landed with in a jeep, bumping and jostling up the mountain tracks. No way out. A whole day in close proximity to some unlikeable companions? No thanks.

As our journey towards sustainable life as a 'real' church continued, some elements of the jeep safari syndrome began to creep in. We began to realise that we were stuck with each other. It has been well observed that relationships move from enthusiastic beginnings to the bump of discovery of shortcomings and limitations. The challenge is then to grow through this stage to acceptance and reality. Certainly the latter was something we strove for in all our dealings with God. We had to learn how to apply it to each other as well. Living with warts in a jeep is probably stretching the metaphors a little far, but I guess that was what it was about. It was time to learn how to live with this person's forgetfulness, that person's incessant chat, his bad time-keeping, her impatience. Then there was his negativism, and her criticism . . . the list, of course, is endless. It does not take much to spark arguments. How were we to survive this adventure, as the uneven track became more noticeable, throwing us against one another, taking us past the beginning friendships, revealing our pains, challenging us to stick together?

Two answers emerged. First, we needed time to explore what travelling as a church family was all about. So to supplement our Square One course, we began Growing Together, an investigation of biblical principles for building healthy church community relationships. This was a home-grown course loosely based on material Graham had picked up. We needed family rules and we needed to find out how God expected us to treat each other. We needed honesty and trust, friendship that would outlast the bumps and knocks along the way.

Most of all we needed commitment. Not to Graham as church leader, but to the church family as a whole. We had to take this seriously, and our studies led us to a desire to express our determination.

So it was that just after our first birthday, we celebrated with a glorious service in the borrowed Maidstone Road Baptist Church. For the new Christians among us, it was time to proclaim their faith. Bishop John Dennis was there to confirm those who had asked for it. Baptist pastor

Jonathan Edwards was there, thigh deep in water as he baptised those who had prepared for it. And then we all committed ourselves to each other in church membership.

'It's just incredible that we have been going for a whole year now.'

'So much has happened—it seems for ever.'

'No! It's gone really quickly.'

Hands plunged in washing-up, minds were free to roam.

'It's so amazing, all that God has done. I just love all the people who love him now, who didn't this time last year. It's so exciting to see.'

Julie was stacking the interminable cups.

'Have you noticed how we seem to have grown in stages—bit like the children really.'

'What do you mean?'

'Well, my kids grow fatter for a while, then taller and thinner. We seem to grow numerically then stop for a bit so new friendships can develop and people get settled in. Then it happens again.'

'Mm, I see what you mean. Though it doesn't apply to everyone. Some folk don't stay with us.' I dried my hands.

'I hate that. I'm sure some just don't like the way we do things, but I worry that we may not have made them welcome enough.' Julie sat down, cupboards all closed now.

'Yet that is harder to do the more we grow. Sounds like a cue for a proper Welcome team and some ridiculous social events.'

So we did.

By this stage, we were nearing the 100 mark, much to my surprise and Graham's satisfaction. So the barbeque went with a swing, and the CCC float for the local carnival was crowded. Huge hands cradled an equally massive

63

globe in the centre of the lorry, and a multitude of national costumes crowded around them. Somehow we squeezed on the band as 'He's got the whole world in his hands' rocked around half of Felixstowe. We even toured some extra streets afterwards, we were enjoying ourselves so much. I'm not sure whether said streets appreciated the volume, but it was fun.

So there we were, literally bumping along together on our vehicle, learning balance while enjoying the ride. Being together, being with God. Learning to love each other through the bumps and jolts, sticking with it even when it was hard.

Yet navigating the tight corners, trying to sing in time with the band, keeping an eye on the children, caring for everyone and everything on our own jeep safari was becoming too much for one person. We formed a team of mechanics—the Pastoral Team—to plan, think and care. Graham was still doing the steering, but now those who had taken on responsibility for areas of CCC's life met together to assist with the maintenance, direction and day-to-day existence of our little jeep. It felt an important move forward.

Perhaps the year-old baby church was growing up already.

5

Developing the Art

It was so very hot. Being under canvas is always worse of course. Being with so many people of all shapes and sizes does not help either. There were times when we simply longed to see the heavy white marquee sides stir in a breeze, but the heat was unremitting, and the air still. Wait! What was that? A movement by the doorway, the beginnings of a refreshing draught? No, too big. The flap lifting, two shadows slipping into the tent. Aha! The Secret Agents!

Summertime at Grange Primary School grounds and two huge marquees dominated the parched grass. Red and black paint splashed the bold message 'CCC Holiday Club'. No fewer than 100 children from the surrounding community squashed into our white haven as we attempted our first such venture. Enthusiasm ran high. Most of us had never done anything like it before, and some had even taken time off work to be involved. The back of the marquee was crowded with makeshift 'dens'—layers of cardboard and blankets—suitable for

THAT'S THE VICAR'S WIFE, YOU KNOW . . .

secret agents and only accessible by password. Musicians raised the temperature even more with all-action, all-bounce songs, while would-be actors ravaged the Scripture Union *Secret Agent* holiday club material to set the scene. Would the two super sleuths solve the puzzle? Would they uncover for the Pharisees what Jesus was up to? Would they find out what really happened that first Easter week? Would they crack the code? Not without a lot of help and plenty of audience participation. At top volume of course.

I'm not quite sure how I got roped into wearing a voluminous black cloak, black hat and magnifying glass in all that heat, but the children seemed to enjoy it. We ran for a week, every morning, with some afternoon games thrown in a couple of times for good measure. Alison was the boss.

It was amazing that we managed to get a project of that size off the ground in under three months. It was lots of fun and yet I sensed God's peace too—it felt as if we were working on his agenda. Actually it didn't seem hard work, even though we were tired by the end. One of the best bits for me was seeing people discover gifts they never knew they had; and doing things they never knew they could. And it was really good to be working as a church towards one aim. It drew us all together. Not to mention all the contacts with all these children and families. I love it.

The children must have enjoyed it as they kept coming back each day for more, despite the heat. The little 'talking corner' saw not a few sneaking off for a chat about this God thing, or perhaps something they were worried about. Then on the Thursday:

'It's just too hot for games today, let's cancel it.' Murmurs of agreement.

'Let's have a prayer time instead. We could all do with some renewing of resources.'

So we gathered round God's word, and then prayed for each other.

Bang! Ann suddenly fell backwards. The rest of us jumped. There she was laid out on the floor. Two people dropped their prayer stance and rushed over to her, concerned, just as—wham!—down went Steve. He was joined pretty smartly by Linda, though with more of a graceful wilt. Alison kept the prayers going while others hovered over their prone companions.

'Are they all right?'

'Is it the heat?'

'Should I get some water?'

Well. God was surprising me again. Was this really a good moment to introduce folk to some Holy Spirit activity? After all, some of the helpers were barely Christians.

Hastily we tried to reassure worried workers that this was God's doing, and that the three on the floor honestly would not be bothered about a glass of water right now. God is blessing them, just wait and see.

Somewhat hesitantly, prayer resumed. We had asked for refreshing after all, and the three certainly looked happy. There were no more outward signs of drama, but lots of buzzing minds. What was this all about? As our time of quiet drew to a close and our inert friends slowly sat up, it was time to ask.

'So Linda, what was that all about? Lesley thought you had had a heart attack.'

'Oh goodness no! I feel so much better now actually.'

'What do you mean?'

'Well, I have been really nervous this week doing the holiday club. It has been so hot too, and I think I've got a bit stressed wondering if I'm doing it right. These things don't come very easily to me. I really want to do them, but they are a bit of an ordeal. And just then, when Alison prayed for me, I felt the Lord meeting with me, and there I was on the floor. I felt all the tension drain away, and the Lord saying to me, "It's OK, I'm in charge, just relax." So I did. I rested in him. And now I feel refreshed, renewed. I can face tomorrow.'

It was so good to see that God had indeed been blessing our companions, and prompted awe among us as we talked about the Holy Spirit.

On the Sunday following the holiday club we held the scheduled services, including a child's christening, in our white-tented temporary home. This was really convenient, as we had nowhere else to go. We had grown too big for Reynolds Court. Grange School had a hall, but the rates were too high. So we enjoyed our canvas worship and then, thoroughly acclimatised, a sizeable group of us trekked westwards the next week for a Christian camping holiday.

Once we reached 'New Wine', sited on the Royal Bath and West showground, we quickly realised how helpful had been our gentle reminder that our sovereign God likes doing things his way, and not necessarily ours. The meetings began, and people were falling all over the place! Not to mention weeping, yelling, groaning, laughing . . . as well as singing and listening of course. The worship band was good, the Bible teaching was excellent and the 'ministry times' extraordinary. Some of our number found it hard to stomach stiff upper-lip British folk behaving in such an apparently abandoned way. Was it all just emotionalism? How could this be anything to do with God? Bishop David Pytches, one of the instigators of the holiday, encouraged us to stick with it and look for results. After all, if it was just stirred-up emotions, there would not be any. He explained what he could, and most of our little party took a deep breath and looked to see what God was doing in all this unusual stuff. Joan's son Andrew was there:

> I have to confess that I was pretty anti all this Christian stuff. I didn't know what to make of all that had happened to Mum and was determined to avoid all the 'New Wine' meetings. I'd heard about all the physical stuff—people falling and shaking and assumed it was all showmanship or something. It sounded stupid to me. Then it started happening to people I knew—I mean ordinary, normal folk. This didn't match up. I talked to Rob about it and decided to risk a meeting.
>
> It was OK, I suppose, and when the time came for prayer I thought I ought to look the part, so closed my eyes and bowed my head. It was weird. Almost immediately I felt a hand on my head though I knew no one was there. Then my eyelids started fluttering. It was as if there was something all around

me, surrounding me. I felt like I had the Readybrek glow! A pressure moved up my hands and arms, my chest. When it hit my stomach I nearly doubled over with it—and yet all the time I felt so amazingly peaceful. The peace was overwhelming. *At that point I heard a voice from the platform saying that God had said that someone called Andrew was being anointed in a special way.*

I was stunned. I came round from the experience feeling that maybe it was true, maybe God and this Jesus bloke were there after all. Perhaps I had been wrong. I was also impressed that if he was there, he was a very personal God. It was a very individual thing that happened to me. I had met someone, not an impartial force. This was the turning point. I had to get to know him better.

Why do we always expect God to do things the way we think he ought? It must be very easy for him to take us by surprise. As our caravan train fought its way back to the east again, not a few of us were somewhat awestruck by God's generosity in meeting with and blessing so many people. Surely he can do anything.

Piles of holiday washing, a mountain of post and an overgrown garden greeted my return to reality. Holidays are always hard to come home from. I want the benefits to stay, the relaxation to continue, but it never seems to happen. Graham was soon back on the phone again, but this time with good news: 'Hey, guess what! Grange School have reduced their hiring rates—we can meet there from now on.'

Our nomadic existence had found a reprieve, and we were back in business. More children were coming, some without parents. More helpers were needed for the Den Gangs, not just for teaching and fun, but for appropriate worship as well. There was a singers' rota, a coffee rota. There were chairs to transport and put out. Music to rehearse. Tables to organise. Sermons to prepare. Readings to practise. Wires to unravel. The more people who came, the more there was to do. What a wonderful problem to have! We quickly discovered it was OK to let people have a go at different things, to find out whether it was for them, with no everlasting commitment to begin with. So there was some chopping and changing as some, inspired by the Holiday Club, discovered talents for cutting and sticking totally new to them. While others tentatively took to a microphone for the first time for reading or singing. The inevitable catering attracted others. Carole was one of many who discovered unexpected talents:

> I came along to CCC because I was attracted by the freedom in worship. I don't mean just the music. I experienced a new freedom to be myself, to be me and worship the way I wanted to. I also appreciated the family atmosphere, and so did my children.
>
> What I didn't expect was to take on and enjoy the production of the church magazine. You see, English was never my strong subject at school, so it was the last thing I would have imagined myself doing. My husband Rob is also working hard on his music in order to help with the worship. God has developed gifts in us we didn't think we had.

Through all the organisation, we tried to hang on to our priorities—reality with God through worship, preaching and fellowship—and that included the children.

It was not always a success. We tried an all-age communion service and it did not really work. Coming from so many different backgrounds, it was hard to know what to do with the children. It was impossible to sweep away centuries of Anglican tradition of wait-till-you-are-confirmed-dear by spontaneously including them in the receiving of bread and wine; yet equally unthinkable to leave them out. It was a bit of a muddle, so we decided to have communion while our younger members were at

Den Gangs, so we had time to think it through. Many Church of England churches are experimenting with children taking communion. Maybe we would join them in the future.

It was all part of establishing our very own identity. As the late summer hazes gave way to autumn colours, our little community accustomed itself to life at Grange School, and began responding to the next challenges. Robert and Lesley bravely began a youth club, meeting in their home. The younger ones wanted a group too, so the Blyford Bunch descended on our house once a week. The Ladies' Group was still functioning in the daytime, but after Square One and Growing Together, what was next? The need to meet together, discuss, learn and pray for one another in small groups became even more important as numbers increased. Homegroups were the obvious answer. We kept the two original courses on a rolling programme for new people. Co-ordination with other churches continued to be important, and occasional joint services were in order.

Then there was the food. The preoccupation did not die, so any excuse was fine, including a Harvest celebration, November bonfire, and a Hallelujah party again to rival Hallowe'en temptations. It even infected our second Tearcraft event, with lunches and snacks as well as crafted goods on offer.

This kaleidoscope of new activities and growing priorities inevitably took its toll on Graham and me. It was definitely time to explore the concept of shared leadership. Our prayer life received a boost as we struggled to keep the channels open between heaven and earth. It had to be the right people. We needed a more formal, permanent structure than just the Pastoral Team, so between us we hammered out a two-fold proposition: a Forum and a

Core Group. The Forum was to be our decision-making body, equivalent to a PCC, to consist of ex-officio members with specific responsibilities (children's work co-ordinator, treasurer, etc), elected members plus three of the Core Group. The Core Group was the second part of the idea, a leadership team to offer spiritual oversight and share in the general steering of the church. So the Forum was set up and after much deliberation and some hassle, the Core Group was initiated with seven members. Between us we hailed from Anglican, Baptist, Roman Catholic and Free Church backgrounds, so it felt a fair and representative group. At this early stage in our church's life, it felt appropriate for Graham to do the inviting as it was his leadership we were sharing, after all. We soon discovered that we brought a range of passions and gifts to our Core Group meetings, and not just backgrounds. At times we were predictable—but God used us all to achieve his purposes!

Graham	I have a brilliant idea.
Dave	Is it biblical?
Ivan	Ah, but have you thought of this problem with it?
Me	Will it help people to grow? Will it help mission?
Steve	We need to pray about this. What is God saying?
Ali	If it will impact and benefit our community, let's go for it!
Ann	What about the pain?
Graham	OK, OK . . . let's talk.

So they will kill me for the caricatures, but that is how it was, and God did help us to work together, to listen to each other, and between us to move forward.

But, there was pain. Ann was right. In all our forward thinking, she was often the one who picked up when people were struggling. She more than anyone brought to the forefront of our identity a concern for those among us who were hurting, and her antennae would distinguish the smallest cry for help. This was a hard-won skill:

I did not come from a Christian home. My parents were against Christianity and I was converted suddenly at sixteen years old. This meant that there were rows every time I went to church. The day I was baptised we had three-quarters of an hour's sleep the night before because we were arguing about it. My mother thought baptism was heresy. She picked up my Bible, the only one we had, and threw it in the boiler. I don't claim to understand this but the Bible didn't burn. My mother and I stood and looked at the Bible and then drew it out. I still have that Bible. Our God is a God of miracles.

That was the first thing that happened to show me that

God is there in the middle of pain. In my twenties I started going out with Ivan. I knew it was wrong because he wasn't a Christian so I didn't talk to the Lord about it. While Ivan was away on a Boys' Brigade camp I had time to think. I loved Ivan but I didn't feel happy about our relationship so I ended up praying, 'OK Lord, I know that you have got to come first. I will finish it.' It was an agonising decision. Two days later I received a letter from Ivan telling me he had become a Christian at camp. The time it happened was the exact hour that I told the Lord through my tears that he was first in my life. It was amazing. We knew at that point we would get married.

My mother died of cancer, and the day before the funeral the Lord actually met with me in the sorrow. He didn't take the grief away but there was a rainbow in the sky and I looked at it and thought of God's promise. I thought, he must be with me now, and utter, total peace flooded me. It was like being baptised in peace. The normal bereavement did not stop but the Lord was in it with me. He was able to meet with me in the pain at a level which no one else could.

Ivan and I found out soon after we got married that I was unable to have children. Childlessness is a bereavement. There is no body or funeral, but that does not make it any easier because the grieving can go on indefinitely. People do say silly things too. I found others' reactions to our childless state hard to handle. In the end I closed up. I went away to retreat twice a year to a local convent. Here the Lord sorted me out. He said he wanted me to give to him my maternal instincts. It was very hard to do as I was scared of being left empty. It was such an enormous part of me. But when I did the Lord just filled me with more and more of himself. I felt I should do a counselling course, and through it found that Jesus was with me in the childlessness, not outside of it. I found that there is a lot of motherhood in God in the way he tenderly looks after us. I have grown more as a Christian through being childless than any other experience of my life.

After the counselling course I went to a charismatic conference with John Wimber which was really good. Before the
afternoon meeting I found myself in tears, but didn't know
why. I wasn't upset. When I asked God about it I looked
down from the balcony and it wasn't the outside but the
inside of people I saw. They were Christians but they were
hurting and bleeding. It lasted a few moments. The Lord then
said to me, 'What are you doing about this?' This changed
my attitude towards counselling completely. I wanted to be
with people in their sorrow and pain as Jesus had been in
mine.

A verse in Psalm 63 sums up my faith and my two-way
relationship with God. It says: 'My soul clings to you, your
right hand upholds me.' I cling to him and he does the rest.

Ann's trained and willing counselling ministry gradually
encouraged others to care and listen. There were several
of us prepared to meet and pray with people on a regular
basis, and Ann gradually grew a full-blown ministry team
from our humble beginnings. Prayer and counselling
became an important part of our identity. Prayer with
anyone who wanted it. We had seen it make a difference.
Counselling for those who wanted help to work on a
painful or disabled area of life. It could take time, but God
was faithful. We had had so much encouragement along
the way. God is God. He can change things. He really does
love us. It was often after the talking—and I do not mean
to underestimate the value of that—when time came for
prayer, that things happened. If prayer is encountering
the living God, then why should we be surprised when it
proves dynamic? I cannot resist some examples.

There was Mandy, who was determined to use her year
out between school and university for God:

I really wanted to do something useful. I wanted to work
with a mission that combined evangelism and practical

action. I knew I needed to grow in my faith as well, so I wa
hoping to work in a team. It was hard to know which organisation to investigate when there were so many good ones. I
wrote to seventeen originally, but three seemed to stand out,
of which Youth With A Mission was one. I didn't know how
I was going to find out which one was the right one for me
and I was in such a muddle. I asked Graham to pray with me
about it. Together we asked God for three specific signs to
help me. The first was that someone would mention the
name of the right organisation without knowing my situation. The second we left to God, and the third was that I
would know inside myself which was right.

After the prayer, I waited to see what would happen.
During the following week, a family friend asked me about
my plans for the year. When I replied that I wanted to work
with a mission, she immediately recommended Youth With
A Mission, as her grandsons were out in Bolivia at that
moment with them. My first sign.

Later that same week, I was flicking through a book by
Adrian Plass trying to find my place when it fell open at a
page where YWAM was mentioned. I was so surprised. This
was my second sign.

The third answer to prayer was harder, as I was still
anxious about making the right decision, despite my signs.
But a friend encouraged me to step out in faith and go on a
YWAM selection weekend. Once I got there, I really liked the
people and the way they worked, and from then on, I knew
it had to be YWAM and was desperate to be selected.

I knew now that if this was the right organisation for me
then it would be OK. I was still really thrilled when I heard
I was chosen to train and work with a YWAM team. We
began in Edinburgh, and then worked in evangelism and
with churches and children's homes in none other than
Bolivia, together with my friend's grandsons. Though we
had hard times as well, all in all it was a fantastic experience.

It was a wonderful answer to prayer.

Then there was an old friend of mine, an occasional visitor to CCC, for whom counselling within our church was a life-changing experience:

> I had been a Christian for many years before I realised that there was a big, painful area of my life that I would not let God touch. For a long time I battled to keep my defences up, but eventually I gave in. I could not hold my emotions down any longer, so a friend from CCC and I arranged to meet and pray about it all. This was a big step for me as I had not talked to anyone before about what was troubling me. I knew I was safe with my friend, and that everything I told her would be completely confidential. This was very important as the burden I was carrying concerned prolonged physical abuse I had suffered as a teenager. The details don't matter, but I was seriously affected by what had happened, even though for years I tried to ignore it. But now I had to face up to it all, I could no longer deny it, and I needed the support of someone I trusted as I began to unearth deeply buried memories. This was an excruciatingly painful process, and I cried a great deal as we talked. The hardest thing about it was that it involved members of my extended family. I think I would have found it impossible to acknowledge without knowing that I had the love and encouragement of both my friend and God. My friend suggested that we pray about each and every incident as I remembered them, and it was while in prayer that I realised just how hurt and angry I was. It was such a release to express how I felt, and I understood why I had been so tense about it all when I experienced the strength of all those powerful emotions.
>
> Once I had been given this freedom to cry and shout and tell God how I felt about it all, my friend gently encouraged me to look towards forgiving my tormentors. At first, that seemed an impossible task. They did not deserve forgiveness, and I could not give it to them. Every time I tried to forgive, more pain and resentment came out. My hands were

clenched in anger all the time, and I hadn't realised how much bitterness and fury I had been holding inside me for so long. We prayed and prayed, and I cried and cried. It took a lot of work, but eventually I got to the place where I could genuinely say that I *wanted* to forgive. We were in prayer at the time and I distinctly remember a physical sensation, as if something passed over me, as I finally said to God that I forgave those who had sinned against me. When I lifted up my head, I found that my hands had uncurled and all my rage had turned to dust. The relief was indescribable. I felt as if a huge weight had been lifted. I was free. I had been like a caterpillar wrapped up in a cocoon of self-protection, unable to move, but now I was released, I was out. The butterfly was liberated. All my strength had gone into keeping my cocoon intact, but now I was free. It was a glorious feeling. Suddenly all the barriers between me and God were down as well and I was free to pray, free to read the Bible with a new enthusiasm, and free to be me.

I have not looked back since that experience and have even found the compassion to pray for those who injured me, as I realise that they too must be damaged people to have resorted to violence in that way. But I needed the time, space and support that the counselling sessions gave me in order to make the journey to freedom.

The more we saw of God at work in people's lives in these ways, the more we wanted to see. There seemed to be times for all of us when we needed the time and prayer support of one another.

God was to challenge Ann and Ivan to further areas of ministry. They both started theological study and, much to their surprise, found themselves called to non-stipendary ministry. They both eventually became Local Ordained Ministers in our parish, widening the scope of their leadership potential and strengthening our church.

God had surprises in store for me as well. My inner battle to trust him over my wretched teeth—and they were certainly looking rather wretched by this stage, as the front two loosened and stuck out even more—had continued pretty much unabated. I had forced myself to ring a couple of other dentists, one of whom had advised a second opinion, but it was no good. The terror that had crept into the back of my mind had me in its fearsome grip, and I was too scared to go. Just the thought was excruciatingly frightening. It is hard to describe, and in the cold light of day I knew it sounded ridiculous, but there it was. It seemed God was big enough to build a church from naught, but not to deal with this.

Sunday evening, communion service in our lounge. A time of quiet, for anyone to pray. A time to listen to God, which is always a bit of a risky thing to do.

'I know it sounds daft, but I have got to say it. Every time I try and pray, I keep seeing this picture of yellow plastic gloves in my mind. Sorry, that is really silly.' I felt embarrassed as I spoke.

There was a pause. Then it was Gill:

'No, no it is not. I work with yellow plastic gloves on at the supermarket, and ever since I have been praying, my hands have been tingling. I think God's been saying I am to pray for you, Di.'

Help.

Gill negotiated the chairs between us and quietly prayed for me and my healing. Nope, I did not feel a thing. Not physically, anyway, but my emotions and thoughts were firing like rockets: 'I am trying to ignore this thing, God. I just cannot face it. I do not know what to do. I do not want to think about it. I want it to go away. Why, oh why has it all gone wrong?'

Well, that really stirred things up. So when we next met

with some friends from Ipswich—the ones who had prayed with me so many moons ago, when I first heard the frightening diagnosis—we talked about it.

'So what is the worst thing in all this?' It was perceptive Pippa who asked.

'The fear. It is the fear.' My stomach knotted even as I confessed.

'OK, we'll pray about that then.'

My tummy convoluted completely. I did not want to pray. It was too frightening.

'Father, please release Di from the fear of what is happening. . . .'

It was an enormous struggle to agree with their prayer. How could I be released? The fear was part of me. However, as their prayers gently but firmly addressed my tortured state, I realised that I did at least *want* things to be different. In that split second, I finally saw the fear for what it was, an interloper, a stranger, an impostor where trust in God and peace should be. Even as the moment passed, and darkness closed in again, I thought I heard the voice of God: 'Stand up.'

Puzzled, the words revolved in my mind. What did that mean? I opened my eyes said and thank you to our friends, feeling a bit shaky. We moved on to other, safer topics for conversation, and we had a good, encouraging time together.

Afterwards, I felt a bit brighter. The words I thought I had heard stayed with me. Stand up. But that was the whole point—I could not. I was down and out, muddied, exhausted and quite unable. Flattened. The command persisted.

Then it hit me.

To stand up meant refusing to allow this ghastly situation to dominate and ruin my life any longer. It meant refusing to take it any more, absolutely disallowing the opposition to rule any more in my mind. I would *not* be messed about with any longer. I would *not* be bullied, cowed, tripped. I would not have it. It would not spoil my life again, not to mention my husband's. Enough!

With a resolution, trembling yet, I set out to visit David Bellamy, a Christian dentist in town (someone had recommended him after a prayer time). He had been warned I would be a bag of jelly, and treated me accordingly. I took Graham along, hardly believing I was being so bold. I tried not to feel afraid, and this time it was different. I was certainly terribly nervous and vulnerable, but not scared witless. I did not even look for the forked tail.

'Well, Mrs Archer, let me explain. Yes, you have advanced problems here. Hardened plaque on the roots of your teeth is setting up irritation, causing gum disease and bone loss. But it is not irretrievable. With careful hygiene and cleaning we can keep your teeth.'

'Pardon?!'

'What we would do is scrape out the offending plaque under the gum line. As long as we keep that under control, the problem should not get any worse.'

Music to my ears, or what?

'Are you sure?'

I told you he was patient with me.

'You do not have to have replacements unless you want them. Understanding of this problem is increasing all the time.'

I could not believe it. Did he really mean it? I could keep my teeth and keep the problem under control? Could it be true?

'I would advise a first treatment soon, and we will get you going with dental floss and mouthwash.'

As it turned out, the treatments were pretty bloody affairs, but I coped, a miracle in itself. The celebration in my soul was unstoppable. Freedom coursed like wine through my being. It was over! I was out! The trap was sprung, the day dawned. I was free! Fear was no more. God did care. He had not deserted me.

OK, so everyone else already knew that. But I had lived with a battered faith for so very long. But now I was healed, and in the end it was my emotions and faith that counted. It was not what happened to my teeth. I had desperately craved physical healing, but it was my emotions that were in the real danger.

'I think, Mrs Archer, that I will have to take out one tooth at the back which is past repair.'

That's all right. I know it's for the best. If I had come to you sooner. . . . It is just so good to be sitting in your specialised chair and know I will never again fear an ejection into outer darkness.

'We are doing well here, we seem to have stopped the rot.'

I thought so. Not the most beautiful specimens in the world, but still mine.

'Bit more cleaning out to do this visit. . . .'

I can't believe I am doing this. This man is an angel. I would swim the Channel if he said it would be good for my choppers. How can this feel safe?

* * *

'Mum, they are great!'

'Oh Mum, you do look different. I think I like them.'

'They are really pretty. A vast improvement.'

Suddenly, it was not a big deal any more. I was free to choose, and after a while, neat plastic teeth seemed like a really good idea. Hardly believing I had come so far I decided to ask for replacement teeth for my two unsightly front ones. My excellent dentist made it as easy as possible. I took the plunge. And it was not long before we were all laughing at how terrible the old ones had looked.

Isn't it amazing what God can do?

6

Things that Cannot Be Said

'But if we walk in the light, God himself being the light, we also experience a shared life with one another, as the sacrificed blood of Jesus, God's Son, purges all our sin' (1 John 1:7, *The Message*).

It was breath-taking. I had expected so little and seen so much. A community of believers, each with a story to tell, where nothing had existed before. God creating *ex nihilo*. Men, women and children amazed and excited to discover that God is real, and real for them.

Perhaps that's why the major ructions hit so hard. I should not have been surprised of course. I should have expected them. We are only human after all and we can be quite ridiculous. We run after so-called fulfilment without noticing the price tag. We so easily imagine it is only what *we* think that matters.

I knew all that. I knew how often our pains and hurts drive us into impossibly painful situations where it is hard to tell who is hurting most. What I did not know was how it felt to be responsible in some way for a growing family of God who were damaging each other.

And of course, I cannot tell you about it, can I? Quite apart from libel, I cannot reopen old wounds, or jeopardise healing that still goes on. For example, if one of our members had had an affair, I could not mention it, could I? Or if someone was struggling with a gay relationship, I cannot say, can I? If a precious marriage broke down, if a Christian child was caught stealing, if a mother committed suicide, it just would not be on to name names. I could not tell you.

You would just have to guess.

The vague suspicions. The half-acknowledged thoughts that all was not well, quickly pushed away. A sense of unease, impossible to pin down. A minute nagging inside that would not quit.

Then the phone call, or the distraught visitor. Or maybe not distraught. Maybe the only sign is nervously twisting hands. After all, it has all been hidden so well, and only a bit of the story comes out now. Is it a husband's suspected unfaithfulness? Or perhaps some evidence has been found. Then again, maybe it is the guilty party sitting there trying to find the words, wanting to call a halt, knowing the whole thing is about to blow. Sentences are difficult, eyes will not meet yours. Shame and confusion wrestle uncomfortably with pain and longing. It seemed such a good idea at the time, everything fell into place. God wants me to be happy, doesn't he? I was, for a moment. Yet now it is turmoil.

It depends of course. Sometimes you are the only one to know. That is bad enough. The worst is when the ground opens inexorably under your feet as the truth begins to spill. The ramifications are painfully obvious. Not just family members and close friends, but implications for the life of the fellowship as a whole, even if most of them never know what happened.

Your heart aches for the person in front of you. It twists for the children, the innocent ones. It pounds in anger at the injustice of life, the sweet fragrance of sin that cloys and erodes, the broken dreams, shattered lives. You want to build, encourage, nurture. Yet this seems only to destroy and cripple. You have seen the kingdom of God on earth, it really is only a breath away. Yet this darkness threatens to engulf the light as if it had never been.

So there you are. You offer a listening ear and comfort and then what? If it is blatant wrongdoing that brings unmitigating distress flailing in its wake, do you rush in and turf the offending parties out? Protect the family of God? But these are people you have worked with, shared meals with, grown to love and care for. It would be so much easier to be fuelled by righteous anger and sort things out, once and for all. But these are not children to be smacked and banished, these are your brothers and sisters in Christ. Even when they cannot see the damage they are causing, you know that day will come. Sin just does not work very well long term. It catches up. So you are torn in an agony of care and responsibility. This cannot be allowed to affect the fellowship any longer, yet you want nothing less than for the offending ones to be restored to wholeness and true freedom, peace and contentment. Bashing them over the heads with the rule book rarely seems to accomplish that. So you try to stay calm, try to keep cool. But the grief is real, and the protectiveness. You are only human too. Your prayer life takes on new dimensions as you plead with the Holy Spirit to do what you cannot—bring back harmony, solve the unsolvable.

And if it is one of those situations where hurt and pain

have just taken over, not obviously anyone's fault, just a consequence of living in this sometimes dangerous world, what then? When the problem is just too big, and breakdown of relationships inevitable, how do you carry that? When the unthinkable occurs, when the wolf gets in and ravages the sheep, who would be a shepherd?

When you pray and pray, and it all gets worse. When you do what you can to get alongside the hurting and the hurter, and still you lie awake at night, tussling with fear for the future. What can you do to stop this mess getting any worse? Yet you have to tread softly. God has not made us judge over one another, and you do not want to lose your brother or sister. Oh for wisdom! When to act, when to pray, when to keep silent.

No, you will not get it all right, by any means. And at the time it may feel that you have lost one or two overboard in the midst of the storms. Only time will tell whether that is true, or whether actually God is more able and more faithful than you ever give him credit for, and that maybe when the waves still and the wind drops you will discover the ones you thought lost are still clinging to the side. In the end they are not—thank God!—your people, but his people. There will be those who come to heartfelt remorse and repentance, and who want desperately to come back on board. And then there is nothing quite like putting the oar back in their hands, and seeing them row with a determination they never had before. Which of course, has an effect on the rest of the boat. If the impossibly bad can happen, so can the impossibly good.

There are those who will surprise you. As you steady the course, recover from the furious squall, and scan the horizon, you will see someone waving to you from another boat. To think you had mourned his drowning! Another church, another chance.

So you go on. There are a few now, crouched in the bottom of your boat, too weak from pain and injury to help pull against the swell, but still with you. Gradually, those pulling the oars learn to take turns to care for this beleaguered huddle. Who knows whom it might be next? Some are slowly restored to health and strength, and take their place once more. Some seem to have been so badly hurt that you doubt whether they will ever be whole again. Yet they are here. Yet you have seen that the light will not be put out by the darkness, so you continue to hope.

Suddenly the boat tips. Bodies thrown against each other, ropes and oars wrenched out of hands. Splash! It rights again. Now what? Eyes peer over the side. In the thrashing water a few heads are visible, arms striking out against the waves for a distant ship.

'We do not like the way you are doing things.' The voices carry over the breeze.

'We are getting out. We think you are going the wrong way. We do not want to, honest. We are really sad. But we are sure you are going to capsize us all on the rocks eventually.'

Off they go. Pleading and discussions are of no avail. They are utterly convinced you are on a shipwreck course. They are too afraid to stay.

Check the maps, the compass. Feel the wind. No, it looks good. Everything in order? Any frayed ropes? Rotting boards? No. Nothing. It is OK. Why then did they go? You stare at their retreating heads, confused. They must be hurting too. It is not easy to jump ship, especially in mid ocean. Yet they leave behind a sense of betrayal and desertion. You sense jagged emotions as you wonder how to carry on friendship with them when you next meet. The holes they leave behind seem enormous. Who will fill them? Confidence is shaken, and it is hard to go on.

'Hey, leave that compass alone. I cannot see it with your head in the way.'

Captain speaking. There are a couple of people who are still here, but who want a go at navigating. They have some valid insights and ideas about the way forward, but are spoiling it by insisting on steering with the boss. They will not let go. Oh great. Why on earth anyone would want to have that responsibility seems inconceivable, but they are at it again. Are they power hungry or just too enthusiastic? Again the cry goes up to heaven for wisdom and discernment. As gently as possible, rogue hands are eased off the tiller. One owner jumps overboard, disillusioned. The other mercifully settles down again to minding the jib sail. She is so good at it too!

Then there are a few who just will not leave the captain alone. Who want to check every detail with him, who would occupy his every waking hour if they could. Compassion mingles with frustration—no amount of time-giving seems to make any difference anyway, so what to do? This is really hard. We all need each other, we all need undivided attention at times.

Yet no one person can be the total answer to another's problems, especially when that problem has been stretching down the years, tangled up in personality, souring world-view. But it is hard to say no. It goes against the grain to set boundaries and limits on our time and giving. It almost seems blasphemous when our God is all-abundant generosity and the ultimate 'Yes!'

Then again, Jesus did find—or rather make—time to withdraw from the demanding crowds who followed him. Time for himself and his Father in heaven, but—he never turned anyone away. It is back to wisdom again. Wisdom to know how to express love—how to seek the best for others. Slowly, it dawns that the giving of our unlimited time and attention is not going to be the best. In the end, it is more that your friend needs. It is the touch of God. That will change lives. Surely the adventure so far has demonstrated that, if nothing else.

Which brings me I think, to the moment to ditch the boat analogy, and to be a bit more honest. I think that I can safely now tell you some things, so you can stop guessing. And in your imagining of some of these things that may or may not have happened, because it would not be fair to say, please do not imagine any criticism. Though it may end up that we are not all in the same boat, we are all fallible, needy humans, and I hope you have picked up my own awareness of that. The warts remain.

Also, I would like to give credit to my husband who,

like many in church leadership positions all over the world, somehow manages to keep his head and weather the storms. However he is still human. When he was training to get his collar turned round, one thing he was told was not to have friends in the church. It causes too many problems.

Now, I have to confess that we have found this impossible to obey. We like to think we are open to all. But inevitably there are those with whom we 'click' more than others. We need support, companionship and love just as much as the next person. Our children need normal friendships with others, just like any other child.

But I wish we did not.

'You only picked him for that job because he is your best friend.'

'No. He is the best person for it.'

'You know about William don't you? After all, you see so much of each other.'

'We do not actually. We are just friends when we get the chance.'

'We thought we would leave you in peace. You must get invited everywhere.'

'Thanks chaps! Wouldn't that be nice.'

So they were right after all. Friendships for clergy, or leaders, do bring problems. But I cannot survive without them. This being human bit keeps getting in the way.

So we try to be sensitive. We try to treat everyone the same, but there are times when only someone who really understands you will do.

*　　*　　*

There are other ways of reminding people that you are human, however. The vicar is not anyone special. He can have a laugh at himself too.

It is back to the sea again. Sails have shrunk though. This time the captain is windsurfing. It is one of those perfect days. Azure blue sky, sunlight dancing on the waves, sand and pebbles shimmering in the heat. The children luxuriate in the freedom and company, leaving the adults to revel in the warmth of relaxation and light conversation. Or perhaps take a glance at the vicar gliding gracefully towards the shore on Rob's windsurfer.

'Here he comes—look at that. He's angled that just right.'

'My turn next!'

'OK, after—hey! What's happening?'

Mesmerised we watched as the windsurfer, a few feet from shore, suddenly jolted and flipped over forwards. Graham yanked on the arm as the mast zipped through the air, directly at a couple walking arm in arm through the shallows. Bham, thud! A woman's cry. The windsurfer was down, Graham was rushing to the doubled-over woman.

Rob and others also rushed down the beach so as not to miss the action. He had looked such an expert too.

Graham's story, and no one has been able to shake it, is that he actually managed to miss hitting the lady by inches, wrenching the mast to the side as he catapulted off the board. What had hurt her was her companion who, reacting to the imminent danger, had grabbed her around the head to pull her out of the way and given her an almighty whack in the process. So she was not pleased with him, and Graham was crimson with embarrassment that he had caused the fiasco. Not to mention effectively ruined his impressive beach approach. How was he to know there was a rock just there, waiting to snag his daggerboard?

Rob and company struggled to show due compassion,

then exploded in hysterics at Graham's expense once the couple moved on.

It was a shame really that we were out with Rob again, that other time. Sadly, he is not the sort of person to let bygones be bygones, especially if you have done something, well, uncool. I am sure this has happened to many people, but they were not out with Rob at the time, so the whole world did not get to hear about it. After all it was a comfortable restaurant, it looked like a very nice meal, and we enjoyed Indian food. We had been adventurous too, ordering some unusual dishes, checking carefully what they were with our waiter.

Yes, it happened. In Graham's selection were some innocent-looking green bean things. He thought that was what they were. We thought he knew what he was doing. A couple of minutes into enjoying our delicacies and a whole one disappeared into his mouth and down his throat. Seconds later and he was crimson once more as he gasped for air.

'Oh no—help—water! I must have water!'

No preamble—he grabbed each of our glasses in quick succession and downed their contents.

'Chilli!' Gasp. 'It must—aah—a chilli!'

'A whole one—you have eaten a whole chilli?'

'Water! Water!'

He was just eyeing the water-filled radiator on the wall longingly when we spotted the waiter weaving his way through the tables at speed, carting a huge jug of water and making unsubtle fire-engine siren noises.

'Fire brigade to the rescue sir!' How dare he laugh. Graham was not bothered, he was too busy drinking.

It took quite a while to settle down after that. We eventually managed to stop giggling at poor Graham's stricken state, and his discomfiture subsided.

And of course Rob promised never to breathe a word to anyone. . . .

So when it comes to being human, faults, warts and all, I think we do it rather well. I think it is good to show that. It is good to fall off a drum stool occasionally, in the middle of a song, sticks flying, legs akimbo. (Yes, Rob saw it all.) It is good to walk into a cupboard because you thought it was the way out, and bang your head in the process. (Yes, guess who was watching.) It is good because just maybe it will help expectations to become a little more realistic. So that it will not matter if a newcomer to the church, helping out with alterations, inadvertently drops wet plaster down the back of the vicar's neck. Poor Steve was mortified. The rest of the crowd thought it hilarious.

On the other hand, you do have to be careful. There was the after-funeral lunch Graham was invited to. By Rob actually—who also kindly warned Graham that if he spoke to Uncle Ted to remember that he was almost deaf. So thoughtful. And of course it was in one of those lulls in the general chatter that Graham came across dear Uncle Ted.

'HALLO. I AM GRAHAM—IT IS UNCLE TED ISN'T IT?'

'All right, all right. I'm not *** deaf!' barked back the response. The air froze. Crimson was the colour of the moment again.

Enough said. We are still speaking to Rob.

Carefully.

7

Burnout

'Hey everyone, it's ten o'clock. Must be time for breakfast!'

Aren't holidays wonderful? No time pressure, no phone ringing, no doorbells, no schedules—just a chance to get away from it all and relax. Well that is the theory, anyway, and that is what we were looking forward to. Summer '93; the loan of a beautiful house in the country; the company of our long-standing friends, the Morrises; an extensive garden for the children to lose themselves in. The perfect antidote to life in Felixstowe.

'You what?! You're playing cricket *again*?'

Suddenly my toast and honey lost its sweetness as I realised what my husband and Dave were planning.

'Yes, why not? They need an extra, and I enjoyed it yesterday,' Hubby responded, slightly puzzled at my reaction.

From out of nowhere, explosions of anger gripped my insides as the missiles came tearing out in my words.

'Do you realise we have only got ten days together—

the evenings are almost non-existent once the children are down—cricket takes for ever—it's hours and hours—what is the matter with you, don't you want to be with me? How dare you want to go off again! Why are you always going somewhere else? I thought this was our holiday!'

There followed that sort of embarrassed pause as I realised I had ruined breakfast for everyone else too.

Somewhat red in the face, Graham got up.

'I think we had better talk about this. Come on.'

Still rocked by the strength of my internal combustions, I deserted my chilling toast and bemused friends and followed him outside into the penetrating sunlight.

'OK, what's going on?' Hubby demanded. 'What do you think you are doing?'

I am not given to outbursts. We were both shaken.

'I don't want you to play cricket.'

'Why not? I can't let Dave down.'

'That's it!'

'What's it?'

'I can't bear it any longer. We revolve our lives around not letting people down, around others' demands and expectations. I know it matters in Felixstowe what people think of you, because you're like an ambassador for the church—and God. But I really don't care if everyone here thinks you are ghastly for letting them down. I just can't bear to let you go for another five hours. I just can't bear it!'

I restrained myself from stamping my foot with an effort.

Hubby sighed. He was torn. He wanted to go with Dave, yet was aware of my distress. What should he do?

We ended up spending the balmy summer evening together, just us, in a pub somewhere. Out it all came.

Frustration that I had been largely unaware of until uncorked at this morning's meal, now bubbled out unchecked. I never saw him. He was out every morning, every afternoon, every evening. There was no time for the children, no space to enjoy them or do things together. I was clearly low down on his priority list too. Plans were overridden at the sound of the telephone ringing. Everyone else's needs came before mine. Marriage was no fun. Mondays were no day off because he was too tired.

The joyless list seemed depressingly endless. I felt selfish and mean, and yet still the complaints tumbled out. I could not understand it. As we looked back over the Felixstowe adventure so far, I was overwhelmingly aware of how good God had been to us, and of all the wonderful changes he had wrought. Yet here was I, grumbling, moaning and exhausted. It felt so ungrateful, and yet it was real.

Our long-suffering friends were dragged into the debate too, as we realised that many of my painful accusations were only too true. But why? Why would God call us to, and bless us in, something that seemed to cost too much? Was it my attitude that was wrong? Christians are asked to take up their cross daily, by none other than Jesus himself. Was I just not being sacrificial enough?

The answers were not exactly leaping to our attention as we ended our week with the Morrises and moved on for a few days as a family. It really was only a few days which merely served to highlight the fact that neither of us felt ready when the time came to rejoin our church family for the New Wine Christian camping and caravan event near Bath. As we bumped our tiny caravan over the grass to take our place in the church wagon circle, I reflected that we had hit only one major realisation so far.

It was this: how did we know that the way we were doing things was the way God wanted us to? Were we actually living in sacrificial obedience, or were my feelings an indication that we were going wrong somewhere? Was there a difference between a good thing to do and a right thing to do? Even on the eve of our holiday, Graham had received an SOS call from someone, to which he had responded, and I had been happy for him to do so. However this meant that the holiday packing had been left to me and that we had set off later than intended, arriving at midnight exhausted and stressed. The SOS had been valid, but then they happened all the time!

New Wine began with a customary swing. The worship was vibrant and enthusiastic, the teaching and seminars stimulating and challenging. Our own agenda, however, was expanding by the day.

Midweek, Graham was nowhere to be seen. For him, it was not so much a bottle of frustration, but a can of worms that had been opened (if you will excuse the mixed metaphor). He was off, gone, managing to obtain use of a room in the neighbouring Abbey, in which to wrestle. The demands from his suddenly voluble wife crashed down upon an inner turmoil he could no longer avoid. He needed time to think.

Setting up the caravan for another night—home from home really, this constant furniture rearranging—I wondered what he was going through as evening dragged into night. Impossibly late, he returned, too tired to talk. I was left in suspense as the next day he vanished again. Had I triggered all this off? It was hard not to feel guilty and yet the conviction was growing that it was our actions and lifestyle that had to change, rather than our attitudes. While waiting, I asked for prayer which was easy at New Wine because everyone was doing it, so it does not feel quite so risky. A close friend did the honours, muttering in that quiet, unconfident, this-is-probably-way-off-line way that convinces you to listen: 'Brakes—use them!' I was still mulling this over, when suddenly Graham was back.

Squashed in our little metal box, cradling mugs brimming with hot chocolate, we dug deeper into the problems.

'It was good to be away. I am sorry I had to, but I needed the space to think.'

'That's OK. Spill the beans.'

'Well it all seems to come down to expectations, both mine and others. I want to do a good job, right? I want to do this well.'

'Of course you do,' I encouraged. 'And you are very conscientious.'

'The trouble is,' he continued, 'everyone has different ideas of what a good vicar is. I try to meet all those expectations, adding on several of my own as well. So I try to be a good preacher, teacher, evangelist, carer, listener, musician, worship leader, administrator, pray-er, everything. I try to relate well to those inside the church and out. Then when I receive any negative or disappointed reactions, I try harder to be who that person wants me to be. I don't want to let anyone down.'

'Like the cricket.'

'Exactly. I don't want anyone to think worse of the gospel I represent because of me.'

'So you try to do everything and be everything. It's never ending! It sounds like housework.'

'Well in a way I think it is. There never seems to be a point where I can say the job is done and finished for the day. There is always more.'

'And you are always full of new ideas.'

'I know, I know. There are never enough hours in the day for me. But I don't think that's the main problem. It is the business of trying to fulfil everyone's expectations that is driving me nuts—and pushing you out.'

'So . . . the million-dollar question. What's the answer?' Hubby brightened at that point.

'Well I thought I would see how Jesus handled it!'

'What do you mean?'

'I thought I would go through the Gospels to see how he handled the expectations of others. I never got further than Luke. It's amazing!'

'Why?'

'Well, it seems to me that he didn't bother about others' agendas for him at all and went out of his way *not* to fulfil them. They were expecting a king, and he was born in a cattle shed. They expected him to work with the religious leaders and he worked with the outcasts. They expected him to stay and minister to the crowds and he went off to be alone. They expected him to lead an army and he was killed by one. They expected him to stay dead, and he didn't.'

Jesus was the Son of God. So maybe he had a better grasp of his identity and task than we did, but the point remained. He refused to be dictated to by others' expectations. He did what he came to do. Were there people who felt let down? What about those in Nazareth who were not healed? What about the others by the pool of Bethsaida? What about those who believed in a politically liberating Messiah? Mary and Martha before Lazarus was raised from death? Surely they were disappointed, confused and even angry with Jesus?

If it was OK for Jesus, did we have to learn it was OK for us too?

It was a tough one. As we faced the long pull across

country to Felixstowe again, the seeds of new principles had been sown in our minds, but the life was yet to come.

I think he was back at work for just three days. That was all it took.

He could not sleep, did not want to eat, wanted to be alone, shouted at me.

It was at this point that our local Ordained-Minister-in-training, Ivan, stepped in. Even without his years of management experience he easily diagnosed: 'Stress, Graham. You have to stop. If you were my employee, I would give you six weeks off. Put the brakes on.'

The brakes! Of course. It was a struggle because they were rusty and the car was used to racing; but there really was no option. The overheating engine required rest. Guilt and responsibility threatened, but eventually the combined pressure of Ivan and Ann Barley, an anxious wife and internal desperation forced the Archermobile off the road, then to stop. The Barleys heroically drove the church on and a five-week break for Graham was announced.

So at last there was time. Time for both of us to acknowledge that the problem was expectations and speed—others' and ours respectively. It was such a vital lesson to try and learn, and once we stopped we could see how we had been overdoing the accelerator. The church had grown so wonderfully, but Graham especially had been trying to keep up with the attendant escalation of problems, administration, ideas and activities to a literally impossible degree. It had all crept up on us unnoticed, but one man cannot do for 150 people what he did for 20. What a way to learn! Those time-out weeks saw much heart-searching as he struggled to get to know the church, the job and himself better.

Strange dynamics fly around the person of the church leader. Especially if he or she has been instrumental in helping someone to find God for the first time, or to take a significant step forward in faith. It seems that we all have an ideal of who we want our leader, or vicar, to be. We each need different things in a leader. It is utterly impossible for one person to fulfil all those expectations.

Teacher, preacher, shepherd, counsellor, carer, initiator, comforter, social worker, problem-solver, figurehead, prophet . . . a leader may be all these things in some measure, at some time. He or she may well be more, but no one can be just what different people would like, all the time. So there will be hurt, there will be disappointment. Disillusionment, even. It is very hard to be the focus of that. If people do not like you, they are likely to leave. If everybody left, there would be no church. There is subtle pressure here then, to be likeable and to want to please. To forget it is God who builds churches, actually.

It was hard work, yet we were both so grateful to have the opportunity to find some answers. We were grateful to the church and especially to Ivan and Ann. It was such a good thing they were there. They helped to give stability in what was an unexpected and unwelcome turn of events for many of our friends.

'So many of us still feel very new Christians,' Lesley mused. 'I don't like this at all. It's horrible not having Graham around. I feel deserted. I didn't realise how much I looked to him. I know in my head that one leader can't answer the needs of all of us, but I guess I want him to.'

Several testified to an initial panic and insecurity. Leaders are not supposed to be ill, they are supposed to be there for the rest of us. We know all too well that leaders are not superhuman, but it would be nice if they were. Just because a leader is the natural focus point, it is so easy to feel important and reassured when he or she pays us attention, and as if we are missing out on the best if they don't.

'But the good thing is,' Lesley continued, 'that we are learning to look straight to God for everything. I think we are maturing. In fact we are managing really well. Perhaps we all have something to learn through this.'

'I don't like seeing Graham struggling,' Keith added, 'because we live as a family in this church, and we care about him. It's not only the loss of our leader for a while, because he's not just a vicar, he's a friend.'

We so appreciated the expressions of love and concern we received during this strange time of wavering between feelings of failure and a sense of liberation. Not to mention all the support from Ann and Ivan.

'Diana, this is absurd—I get home from work at six o'clock and the phone doesn't stop ringing all evening, every evening. It's ridiculous!'

One week into their driving role and the Barleys were horrified.

'How on earth does he deal with all this paper?'

Two weeks and they were adamant.

'He's not coming back to work without an administrator. Somehow the church just has to afford it.'

So it was not just that we were failing then. Someone else thought the load impossible. As we gradually came up for air, it all seemed such a far cry from our chaotic, exciting, God-centred beginnings as a church. And yet it was a time of realisation for many of us.

'I have printed a list of who is responsible for the different areas of the church's life. Then we need not phone Graham all the time.'

'I am enjoying helping with the worship. Perhaps I could carry on?'

We had to take responsibility together for our church. It really was not Graham's any longer. It really was all of ours. We were growing up again.

Then there was Lesley of the itchy fingers. Part-time nursing has lost its appeal and praying about it inevitably produced an interesting sensation. Her fingers began to itch. All she could think of was that God wanted her to use her fingers in her next job. Typing seemed to her to be the obvious answer, and so an administrator was born.

When all too quickly, the five weeks were up and a refreshed if wary Hubby went back to work, the changes were not confined to church life. Having rediscovered the joy of his children's company, he was not about to forfeit it all again. An answerphone was installed, coupled with a general request not to phone over tea-time. He and the Core Group worked hard to share responsibilities better—motivation no problem. Saturdays were not automatically all working any more. It was going to be a whole new regime.

Of course it was not all perfect after that. Of course things still got muddled and difficult. But we know the danger signs now. And I hope we have learnt how to use the brakes at the first sighting.

8

Bishops, Baptism and Bewilderment

'Keeping the window open for ecumenical co-operation.'

It was there in black and white. It was in the contract. The bishop wanted us to be a church for the estates, for all Christians. Not just those who would call themselves Church of England.

Of course, you know it all now. You know about the slippers and the chocolate cake, the soap suds and the smiles. Squashed into our over-used lounge, it would have been hard and have felt inappropriate to use just the formal Anglican liturgy for those first services. We used some of it, but not all, and not all the time. We were keeping the window open.

That was why our initial back-up reference group was ecumenical too, mainly Church of England and Baptist, with others represented for a while.

We were the one church on the estates and we wanted to be open to all. However, this was often easier intended than achieved.

John 17:20—'*I pray for those who will believe in me through their message . . .*'

'We do not want our baby christened. He must wait until he is old enough to make up his own mind.'

'*that all of them may be one, Father . . .*'

'We cannot agree. Our child is part of the family of God as we are. He is inside God's grace now. If he chooses to step outside later on, then is the time for his decision. But we want to bring him up within the kingdom. We want him to be christened.'

'*just as you are in me and I am in you. . . .*'

'Decisions should be made by everybody together. God will guide us.'

'*May they also be in us . . .*'

'We need anointed leadership. That is the way forward.'

'*so that the world may believe that you have sent me. . . .*'

'We are all priests before God. All equal. A communion service is just the breaking of bread together. Anyone can do it. Anywhere.'

'*I have given them the glory that you gave me . . .*'

'I need a proper priest to hear my confession.'

'*that they may be one as we are one: . . .*'

'We need things done decently and in order, like St Paul says in 1 Corinthians 14:40.'

'*I in them and you in me. . . .*'

'We need lots of space for the Holy Spirit to work, for each person to contribute to the service, for speaking in tongues, prophecy, words from God, like St Paul says in 1 Corinthians 14:26.'

'*May they be brought to complete unity to let the world know that you sent me and have loved them even as you have loved me.*'

Was this why Jesus prayed so hard? Unity, brethren,

does not seem to come naturally. Here we were, determinedly holding the door open for all who wanted to come, and then discovering that God indeed took us at our word and drew a thoroughly diverse set of people together. How were we to reconcile passionate differences of belief on such fundamentals as baptism, the basic expression of conversion? Some of those who joined us from the crippled house church at the beginning of our life were mystified. How could we baptise babies when they had made no choice for Jesus? Others were equally confused. Were babies and children beyond the reach of God therefore, until able to speak for themselves? No shortage of biblical backing for either camp. Remember both Lydia and the Philippian gaoler whose whole households were saved and baptised (Acts 16)? Ah, but what about Peter in Acts 2, encouraging all to repent and be baptised? How can babies do that?

There were dozens of issues which threatened, almost taunting us with their ability to create seemingly insurmountable obstacles. Do we have to be Church of England? What about the bishops who do not believe? Yet we must be accountable somewhere. There must be authority. Otherwise if Graham goes off the rails there is no one to stop him.

All this was in addition to the battling for priorities as passions began to develop in people's hearts for areas of the church's life:

Children must come first.

Outreach is a must.

Mission, mission, we have to show the world we care.

Worship has to be good, to draw us closer to God.

We need more in-depth Bible study.

'May they be brought to complete unity. . . .'

It has been one of our greatest challenges. We wanted

to be true to our calling. We did not want to be defeated by impossible problems! We knew of a handful of other churches who were ecumenical in nature, and working. Perhaps joint Anglican and Methodist, or Baptist and Church of England. So it had to be possible.

That first leadership group, the Core Group, was a fair reflection of the spectrum. Anglican, Baptist, Free Church and Roman Catholic. It did not take long to discover that the key was commitment. A commitment to stand together, to keep on working towards each other, no matter what. Not to give up, not to prejudge. To listen. To believe in Graham's vision of crossing as many church divides as possible. Refusing to give in to easy, separating solutions. Then again, not to create something so new that it became just another strand, another micro-denomination, but to honestly pull together what already existed.

There were moments when the task seemed of Herculean proportions. It had repercussions inside and out. Accountability beyond our walls (wherever they happened to be) was a problem. The Suffolk Ecumenical Council was not set up to take responsibility for individual churches. Yet the Church of England had asked us to be ecumenical, so was straightforward accountability to the diocese appropriate? Then again, the local Anglican deanery was supporting us financially, Graham is an Anglican minister. The Suffolk Baptist Union voiced its applause of our venture and later provided a small measure of funds for his salary. What should we do? We had originally been encouraged to set up a Local Ecumenical Project, but this would mean being overseen by six different denominations. Our battles to accept diversity in our midst was one thing, but discovering how to relate to various authorities with their different ways of working was another.

We had a membership list. It gave us local identity.

However, if our members moved location, how would they explain their Christian commitment to another group of believers? Had they been baptised or confirmed? Would they be accepted? Or would they have to start all over again? What did God want us to be?

'I baptise you in the name of the Father, and of the Son, and of the Holy Spirit.'

More services of baptism and confirmation. Alison was confirmed. Her husband Richard was baptised by full immersion in the borrowed Baptist church baptistry by the local Baptist minister. Both the couple had been christened as babies.

> I wanted to be confirmed because looking back over the years since my baptism I could see that God had been there, caring for me, even though I did not recognise it at the time. We had gone to church as a family until my father died, but the vicar then said all the wrong things and we did not go back. So there were many years when I did not consider God to be a part of my life. Then we lost our first baby daughter, Claire, and I wanted to go to church again. Our two boys went to the first CCC holiday club and then we ventured to the Sunday services. Getting to know Jesus for myself has been so special because I now know that there is somewhere where there is no more suffering. I don't know what heaven will be like, but I know that one day in some way I will be with Claire again, and that is important to me. When it came to declaring my newfound faith, it was an intensely personal thing for me. It was for me, not for anyone else, not for public show. I wanted to confirm what God had begun in me all those years ago, when I was too young to understand.

So what about her husband?

> Yes, I was baptised as a baby too, but I didn't really consider that it meant anything. We never went to church when I was young, and I never thought much about God. When Claire

died I went along to CCC with Alison to support her in that awful time, but then gradually discovered Jesus for myself. It was a huge change for me and I really wanted to show that. I didn't feel that my baby baptism had left me with anything to confirm, so I definitely wanted to go for it now. I had found meaning to life at last and the physical act of baptism demonstrated my new, strong convictions.

So how did it go?

Baptism was a real experience! Coming up out of the water I felt joy and peace. It was exciting to belong to Jesus, and it was exciting to belong to the fellowship. There was also a sense of sadness for all the wasted years of not knowing God, but now there was really something to go for in life. The only thing I regretted was that we had to borrow a church for it. It would have been nice to have been baptised in my own church.

What about Alison?

Well, when the actual moment of confirmation came it was over very quickly, though the time beforehand of giving my testimony seemed to last a long time. I was still glad I had chosen to be confirmed. I didn't want to deny what God had been doing in my life all those years when I didn't know him.

Was it any problem to you that you chose different things?

No, that was fine.

So how do you feel about being in a church that offers these options?

It's good—the more choice the better. You can respond the way you want to then.

What about your children, have they been christened?

Well, when the boys were young we responded to family pressure and asked for them to be, but the vicar where we were then would only baptise children from regular church-going families. At the time we thought this was pretty awful but now we can see why he said that, and we're glad. After we became Christians and had our second daughter Kathryn, we decided to dedicate them to God.

Despite your positive experience of infant baptism Alison?

Yes, because that was only with hindsight. This way they are free to make their own decisions without any hassle.

So that was it. We had to make room for God. He works in different people in different ways. We had to leave space for different experiences, equally valid. That was the starting point, trying to meet people where they are. So on a practical level we wanted to offer as much as we could, and for that to be OK. We wanted to learn how to respect one another's experiences and responses to the same God. Hence these services where some are confirmed and some are fully immersed in the water of baptism. Hence the decision to offer parents the choice of thanksgiving and dedication for their children, or baptism.

This also entailed the choice for all of us to respect each other's theology. It was not, and is not, an easy walk. It is very hard when you think someone is seriously wrong. It is excruciating when your own church both upholds your beliefs and practices, and challenges them at the same time. It is so uncomfortable and disconcerting. Yet is it not also realistic about the Christian world? Challenging about what really is important?

It was at that innovative service, where Jonathan Edwards, a Baptist pastor on our reference group, was baptising two and the bishop was confirming three others, that Bishop John Dennis came out with the immortal quote: 'Well, I am not quite sure what we are doing here but I am sure that God is pleased with it.' We have had Bishop John's support for our ecumenical attempts all the way down the line.

Sorting out the implications for our official status is a more complicated problem. Our electoral roll form includes allegiance to the Baptist Union as well as the Church of England, with the aim that eventually this liason will be legal. This could mean transferring our direct lines of authority to Churches Together in Suffolk, whereas they have been to the Church of England up till now—and to be fair, the Anglicans were putting in the cash. So constitutionally there could still be changes to come, but practically we are the body of Christ in this area of Felixstowe, open to all.

Our Growing Together course had helped to define our aims in bringing together different strands of churchmanship and none, and the membership statement is also important:

> As a Christian I seek to:
> know God as my Father;
> follow Jesus as Lord and be filled with the Spirit.
> As a member of the Cavendish Community Church it is my desire to:
> use the gifts and resources God gives me in active involvement within the life of the church and in its mission to others.
> Together with God's help I will:
> fashion my life according to the Bible, be regular in worship, support the leaders, resist the Devil and grow in love for God and his people.

Travelling to the popular New Wine Christian holiday camps has also enhanced our sense of being part of something bigger, and not necessarily Anglican!

We want first to belong to Christ and then to one

another and then to belong to the wider church, as wide as we can possibly make it. When we made our first membership declaration that day, thirty people made a commitment to stand together, those from Free Church, Anglican, Baptist, Roman Catholic and no church backgrounds. It was a good moment.

It is a continuing journey. Every time, for example, an infant is brought to the front for either dedication or baptism, the issues are sharpened again in many minds, yet the obligation is there for us to pray just the same for the little ones. And because we have grown to love and respect one another, genuine friendship spanning our theological differences, it somehow keeps things in perspective.

It is so important to allow our main expressions of faith to unite and not divide us. From shaky beginnings, our celebration of Holy Communion is growing into a very special time—whether it is led Anglican style or Baptist style. We may prefer one or the other, but the important thing is the gathering together around the Lord's table to remember and proclaim his death and resurrection, whatever the levels of formality and liturgy. Jesus asked us to do it not argue over it.

Our commitment to genuine unity received a major boost when a retired Baptist pastor and his wife joined our congregation, and eventually our leadership. Gordon and Iris Whittle brought a wealth of experience with them, as well as a solid Baptist background. They became members of our multi-faceted church, along with people like Steve, who couldn't have been more different.

I had seen him leaning up against the wall. He looked a bit self-conscious, as if he was trying to be invisible. He was a bit wary perhaps, weighing us up. He was friendly but guarded:

I was brought up in the Roman Catholic Church. My family all went along and I was always in church. I served at the altar. God was a big part of my life. My mum especially encouraged us and I used to pray a lot. When I started work on the farm it was harder to get to church, as animals need care seven days a week, but I was still very aware of God, especially in the beauty of the countryside I worked in.

Long-distance lorry driving coincided with a spiritual desert, however. I would have gone right off the rails if it had not been for my upbringing!

Then I met this brilliant girl. She told me straight away she was a Christian, to which I replied I was a Catholic, which to me meant the same thing. Right from the start God was involved in our relationship, and the *Good News Bible* she gave me brought alive the word of God to me in a new way. However, we soon discovered that her Baptist background and my Roman Catholic one clashed all over the place. I didn't know what to do. Which church should I go to? Who was right? When I finally ventured to Alison's church it was a real eye-opener. There were so many differences to my Roman Catholic understanding, yet they were worshipping the same God. Who was I to say I was in the only true church, the only one to have it all right? Lots of my prejudices were destroyed at this point, and I gained a lot from listening to Pastor Don Bridge's sermons there. All the time I was asking questions of God. Which is the right way to do things? What is the truth? Alison and I were to be married, but in which church? I had been taught that the bread and wine of Mass *became* the body and blood of Christ, and we only ever took the bread. For Alison, they *represented* his body and blood— should I take her church communion? This was a huge issue for me, but in the end I couldn't sit on the fence for ever. I felt right with God about it so went ahead with communion. Sometimes I felt I had answers to my questions, sometimes I felt God was telling me not to worry about it, he would deal with it later. So the wedding service was held at her church, with my Roman Catholic priest to give a blessing, and both our families were happy. The important thing for me was that Alison was the girl for me, and God seemed to think so too.

But my spiritual battles weren't over. I could not settle in a church, and often let Alison and the children go to the Baptist church without me. However, she had always had a vision for a local church on the Felixstowe estates where we now lived, so when CCC arrived, she was there. I was still struggling and had no courage to witness at the docks where I worked, no enjoyment in church, and no excitement with God. I was in a real rut.

Then my kids dragged me along to CCC too, they were so happy there. I tried to stay at the back and watch. There were not too many weirdos. I saw the change in my mate Rob, and gradually I got drawn in. I started to feel different inside. My emotions were being stirred and every time I went the sense grew of being on holy ground. I appreciated Graham's leadership, his sticking to the Bible, and his expectation of God to act. This was a church for participants, not an audience. God became important to me again, holy and real. Praying was exciting, life with God was at once relaxing and energising. God's presence was there. Visions and pictures became part of my prayer life.

It was also a church for all. I do not have answers to many things, any more than I did before, but perhaps there aren't any. I believe passionately that Jesus wants one bride, his church, and we belong to it if we love him. I wonder if he is not as legalistic as we can be.

Our children were dedicated at CCC. Both our families came and enjoyed the day. When it comes down to it, I just want to serve God, and grow as a Christian, wherever I am.

'That all of them may be one. . . .'

Clearly it would be a bit useless if we were expending all this energy and heartache among ourselves to be truly ecumenical if we were not speaking to the other expressions of the body of Christ in the rest of Felixstowe outside our estates. It was early on in the big adventure that Graham began to meet with some of the Anglican and Baptist ministers in our immediate locality for weekly prayer. This commitment grew in Walton to a full-blown covenant in June 1991 between three church congregations—two Anglican and one Baptist—to work together wherever possible and support each other. The ministers at the other two churches have changed since, but the co-operation remains. It has expressed itself in various ways. That joint harvest service we had in our first autumn proved the forerunner of other combined activities including evening services, special events, helping with each other's holiday clubs, advertising together for Christmas and Easter.

And the rest of Felixstowe? Yes, we joined Felixstowe and District Christian Council, we were there when it became Churches Together in Felixstowe. When I stop and look at it, we have actually done all sorts of things together as the body of Christ, very happily! There was the open-air service on the beach where we joined in with the Salvation Army and the Roman Catholics, then later the Pentecost 'On Fire' initiatives when it rained like anything, but did not dampen enthusiasm. Then there are the various musical extravaganzas, inspired by the multi-talented Andy Rayner and his cronies, hiring the seafront theatre and drawing Christians from all over town and beyond, to proclaim in dance, drama, songs and lights the Christmas message, or the Easter message, or just the gospel message. Any excuse, but doing it together. Producing an album of contemporary Christian music to raise people's spirits, and cash for Tear Fund or Christian Youth Ministries in Ipswich. Selling Tearcraft goods in many Felixstowe churches, and getting to meet each other.

But now I want to lay out a far better way for you. If I speak with human eloquence and angelic ecstasy but don't love, I am nothing but the creaking of a rusty gate. If I speak God's Word with power, revealing all his mysteries and making everything as plain as day, and if I have faith that says to a mountain, 'Jump,' and it jumps, but I don't love, I'm nothing.

If I give everything I own to the poor and even go to the stake to be burned as a martyr, but I don't love, I've got nowhere. So, no matter what I say, what I believe, and what I do, I'm bankrupt without love. (1 Corinthians 13:1–3, *The Message*)

The sky is clear blue. A light breeze stirs the new leaves bursting from the branches. The traffic is intermittent, not as dominant as usual, though many shops are open. It is different these days.

Tramp, tramp.

Wires snake across the grass. The wind-shelter houses a drum kit today. Spring flower beds are obscured by waiting feet.

Tramp, tramp.

Shoppers' heads turn in curiosity. Microphone stands proliferate and the mixer desk stands opposite the cinema. Musicians are at their posts and all is ready.

Tramp, tramp. Here they come! Not one cross, not two, but more and more! From each corner of Felixstowe, they are marching to the centre, crosses held aloft at the head of each procession. There is the Catholic priest in his eye-catching black cloak. Here is the Free Church pastor, sporting his regulation casual jumper. Tramp. There are even more people than ever this year. Yes, here is the Salvation Army, ready with their instruments. Cross after cross arrives, and the town centre grass triangle disappears under arriving Christians. We spill out over the pavements, and manœuvre to spy the little platform from where our Good Friday service will be led.

Pause. We are all here now. It is time. The band strikes up and here we are, right in the heart of the town, standing together to proclaim our Saviour's death and resurrection to heaven and Felixstowe.

The music goes well, the amplification copes, the singers lead us, and the drama enacts the familiar yet powerful story. It is good to pray too, here in the middle of everything. The preacher, Anglican this year, talks to us and the town. Then there is music again.

I gaze at the jutting roof tops surrounding us. My town. I cannot help getting emotional about this. It is just so very good to be worshipping together here. Jesus is our Lord, the same one. The world has every right to laugh and sneer if all we do is bicker and destroy each other, but when we lift up Jesus together, differences taking second place to unity . . . well.

They were looking that day, as they went past.

Some even stopped.

'that the world may believe.'

9

Tabernacle to Temple

'There is this sort of a lump on the top.'

'Um—a lump?'

'Yes, a lump. A big black lump on the roof.'

'OK. Anyone else?' Graham asked.

'Well, when I was praying about it, I felt that I was looking down over the congregation. Like there was some sort of balcony.'

10th January. Our fledgling church had been in operation for six months now. Which at the time seemed an absolute age. We felt well able to tackle the challenge of what to do with the piece of land sitting over the road, tagged with our name.

Right from the beginning of our short life, it had been a priority. Although donated by the original landowner, Trinity College, Cambridge, for a church, confusion reigned over the little site. 'It is for a community centre, isn't it?' 'A hall, that's what we need.' 'We've got shops, and a field to play on, we need somewhere to meet.' We heard it all. Vague memories of vaguer promises fluttered

around the community, and in the middle we sat, knowing it had been given for a church, and wondering how to delight and not disappoint the estates' residents. We needed wisdom and sensitivity as well as vision.

Number one bright idea was to put a portakabin over there, to be a temporary home for us and proclaim the church's presence. However, even while investigations as to cost and planning permission were under way, more people were joining us, so by our January meeting there was not a portakabin big enough. It was time for some serious prayer. It was a permanent building or nothing.

'It is the first time I've fasted, Graham, and I've actually enjoyed it.'

Many of us had made this day a special one because we really needed to listen to God. What were his plans? Going without food was a way of saying we were in earnest—and it does concentrate the mind wonderfully.

'I think we should go for a permanent, proper building.'

Murmurs of assent.

'Well, there is not room for two. Is it a church or a community hall?' Graham probed.

'We need a church! God has done so much for us, we want others to have the same opportunity.'

'Should it be both? A church on Sundays, and hall on weekdays?' The question had to be asked.

'Not sure . . . no, not sure. But we *are* sure we need a church.'

It was as we were considering our strange triangular piece of land, still obliterated by mud and contractors' cabins while the Safeway store was being built, that the unexpected pictures came. A completed building with a black lump and a balcony? It seemed so unusual, it just might be from God. It could just be an indication of where we were heading. We filed the suggestions away and wondered.

It was at this stage that our nomadic wanderings began. The following month saw our first move to Reynolds Court, as Blyford Way became untenable. Chairs, amps, tea and coffee, OHP projector and screen, children's activity supplies—it all came with us. Unpacking and repacking, cleaning, winding wires, and furniture moving was hard work, but was worth it. The extra space was wonderful, and it was a change to use someone else's sink.

While we were acclimatising, the Safeway builders finished their task and suddenly our site was clear. A minute's wander over the road took me to it. I gazed at the churn of mud and earth left behind by the contractors and felt uneasy. Next to the huge supermarket and sprawling car park it seemed insignificant, minute, and a very odd shape. The triangularish perimeter sloped steeply up to the playing field above on two sides and it was hard to imagine it big enough for a house, let alone church. Yet it was central to the estates, and right opposite the pub.

But how could we, a fledgling congregation, just getting to know God and each other, take on responsibility for a building project? I could not see it. How could we go for imaginative planning when the life and growth of our little church was more than a full-time job already? I felt overwhelmed by that alone. There was enough people-work to do, without bricks and mortar as well.

As I stood looking at that unpromising chunk of soil, hope suddenly stirred. Perhaps that was the key. It was not I or even Graham-and-I any more. It was we. It was us. All of us together. It was not *my* faith that needed to be big enough, it was all of ours. Though Graham would still carry the can, we had to do this together. It had to belong to us all. It was not the same as that original door-opening exercise when the responsibility had been just for me and him. This time the adventure in faith was for us all.

I felt brighter as I turned back towards our house, where it had all begun. Perhaps this was a challenge, not a crushing load. As long as I thought *we* and not *I*. We had to go for it, together.

And so the serious stuff began. First, the research.

Could the site be enlarged at all?

No. Definitely not.

Ah, right. Well, would a two-storey development be possible?

That will take some finding out.

OK, we will do that then. A building team? Yes! A building team.

Six enthusiastic members with no experience of building whatsoever formed our exploratory team. Now we are really getting somewhere. I was not among them, though Graham, of course, was. For me, the together principle had begun. Visits to several comparatively new church buildings were undertaken, as we all tried not to be daunted by the thought of a £300,000-plus project when we had next to nothing in the kitty. Graham tried to boost our flagging faith by reminding us that it is easier to find £300,000 (a reasonable estimate of our needs) for something which fits God's plans than £3,000 for something that does not. I hope he is right.

Then John Cull, the vicar of our parish church, had a suggestion. 'Graham, we are wondering about our daughter church, St Philip's. The numbers there are decreasing, and we think it is time the small congregation should close. We were wondering about selling the land and giving you the money for Cavendish Park. What do you think?'

All that glitters. . . . At this early moment, when we had literally no idea where the money for a building would come from, was this God handing us the solution? Not so fast!

Somehow the local press got hold of it and for the residents of the St Philip's area it really did not sound like such a hot idea. Where would the groups using the hall go? Was it fair to close down the congregation, however small and elderly? What about the area's children who come to the Sunday school? Why move the money out of the area? However, before the furore could really get going, the catch was uncovered. The deeds on the land prevented it being sold or used for anything but a church, so that was that. It was not going to be that simple.

'John—Graham here. Thanks for the thought. To be honest, I don't think I was entirely happy about the St Philip's proposition, but I gather it is out of the question now anyway. We will battle on.'

Then, incredibly, there was real gold. Graham thought it was a call to wish him a happy birthday, but reeled back into the lounge after he had replaced the handset.

'That was Dr Bradfield from Trinity College. They want to help with building the church. Can you believe it—they will give us £100,000 if the diocese will match it. That's amazing!'

'It's not. It's fantastic!'

Talk about encouraging. We were thrilled. We were sure the diocese would back it. £200,000 in a phone call. It was hard to take in. It was so good to have someone believe in our project to that extent. The College were keen for a church that would also provide space for community use. It was clearly time to pursue options.

Yet just then we were also facing an immediate pressing concern. Reynolds Court was now bursting at the seams, and though some of the residents joined us, we were becoming rather an invasion every Sunday. There was only one option left on the estates. Grange Primary School. At first it went well. We moved in at the beginning of July, swapping the lounge feel for blue climbing apparatus, creative work and a hard floor. Gradually, though, tensions began to develop so the governors asked us to move out for the summer period. This was just prior to the first holiday club in the grounds, which went ahead. We felt truly nomadic under canvas, with nowhere to go the following week. After lots of prayers, the chairman of the governors unexpectedly joined us, bringing some very practical ideas about how to resolve the situation. The summer months saw us finding the route off the estate and into St Philip's to meet there, but by the end of September we were back at Grange School, with more rooms available and for a lower fee. A corporate sigh of relief went up, but once again we had been reminded that the church is the people not the building.

Christmas and we were on the move again. In four days we used four different venues: the open air from the back

of a lorry, carol service in the school, midnight communion in our house and Christmas family service in St
Philip's hall. We survived.

In the middle of this silly season, the building team
requested a feasibility study and proposed building plan
from an Ipswich architect. By November the reply was
forthcoming. Beautiful drawings arrived but they bore a
price tag of £500,000. It was back to square one.

I have to confess relief at this point that I was not part
of the building team. Every time I shopped at Safeway, I
tried not to look at our neglected triangle of land, which
often seemed to reproach me with its wild grasses and
scattered poppies, springing up where foundations
should be. Would it ever change? It was probably a good
thing I was not on the team actually, with all this despair
and longing. They just shrugged, growled and started
again.

New Year came and the building team had done their
visiting. We were set to follow the example of others and
invite tenders from 'design and build' companies. We
asked five.

Grange School continued to be our home. Every week
we unloaded all our equipment into its copious rooms.
We were able to grow again (about 120 now) and
attempted to build good links with the school, praying for
its community. It was a good, central base for us, and we
appreciated being there. However, June found some of us
trekking our way to the St Philip's area again, this time
with a different purpose. We were aiming to visit the erstwhile members of the church there to find out how they
felt about John Cull's latest idea. We collected a mixture
of reactions:

'I've been attending St Philip's for more years than I can
count. I know we are only a tiny congregation now, but I

did not want it to close. Why couldn't it carry on? Why couldn't there have been someone to help us?'

'If Cavendish Community Church comes and meets here, it won't be the same will it? I cannot cope with all this bouncy worship. There won't be a place for me.'

'I would like to come along and see what you do, once you have moved in. It will be hard to watch you change the place though.'

St Mary's PCC had decided to close down the congregation at St Philip's and offer the premises to us, to use for the foreseeable future until we had our building on Cavendish Park. They even gave us some money to help with the necessary renovation. The catch was that they also wanted us to share responsibility for the area, representing a mere 3,000 people. This brought the total to 7,500 which was rather daunting for a two-year-old congregation. With prayer and trepidation, we took on the challenge, more aware of limitations than ever.

So this time the people of CCC faced an unusual move. This one was to be semi-permanent, and the premises were to be ours. After all our wanderings, it seemed very strange. Over the summer we knocked poor St Philip's about a bit. There was no option—the two single-storey rooms had to be changed to accommodate us. The original church side we converted and carpeted for the Den Gangs to use, putting in dividers and curtains. The larger hall side now had to double as a church, so we repainted it. Gill and Jim made some beautiful banners which helped it to feel more like a place of worship. By September we were up and running, trying again to acclimatise to yet more new surroundings, but thoroughly relieved to have store cupboards at last. It was wonderful not to have to cart so much around, and great to have somewhere of our own to use during the week and for socials. It was quite a step to now be responsible for the regular hall upkeep and lettings. We were especially thrilled that about ten of the original St Philip's congregation came and joined us, *and* seemed to enjoy the 'bouncy worship' as well as our more reflective moments. Some of the others went to the mother church of St Mary's, but the children kept coming, joining ours in Den Gangs, filling them to overflowing. There was plenty of room, especially in the summer, with the enclosed grass garden round the back. Here we also celebrated Ivan's and Ann's ordination to local priesthood, and they tried to look casual in their back-to-front collars.

And all the time, God was reminding us of what we were there for. The church is the people not the building.

'I always believed there was a God. The idea that this wonderful world is just a chemical accident seems utterly ludicrous to me. But I'd never been to church, I had a family to care for and always worked at the weekends.'

We were sitting in Julie's pretty flower-strewn garden. I had been longing for a chance to hear her story in full. The fragments I had gleaned were fascinating.

'Then we moved, I stopped the work, and decided after a while to give church a try. You weren't a bit interested, were you, Keith?'

'No, not at all.' Husband Keith was there too. 'I couldn't see the point.'

'Well, I went to the open-air service on the green, but actually tried another church for a while with a friend. Then my neighbour Lesley invited me to CCC. I didn't know whether to go or not. The night before I couldn't sleep, I was tossing and turning. Was there a God? Was it true? Is Jesus real? Eventually I prayed in desperation, "God, if you are there, please let me know." Suddenly I felt the warmth of a hand upon my head. It was a very clear sensation. All my turmoil drained away and I thought, "Right, that's it. You are there," and I turned over and went straight to sleep.

'From that moment on, I have been getting to know him. I came with my children to CCC. I listened and watched. Somehow I found myself in the deep end, helping with the Den Gangs. I knew so little, and it was so scary, but this disciplined me to read the Bible and find out more.'

So what did Keith think of all this?

'I have to say that I was not impressed. I think our marriage had been under a lot of pressure with the demands of our children. I often felt pushed out, and when Julie started going to church, it was the last straw. I'm ashamed of it now, but my dislike was pretty intense. It felt to me as if something huge had come between us and I hated it. It hurt me and I lashed out at Julie, refusing point blank any suggestion of going along with her.'

Julie took up the story.

'It was a ghastly time. I was discovering something really precious, that Jesus is real and cares about me, and here was my husband making me pay for it. Our marriage was hanging by a thread. I gave up on him ever finding God like I had.'

Then came New Wine.

'Someone dropped out at the last minute, and Julie and two of our children took their place. I was not happy about it and let her know it in no uncertain terms. My son and I were left on our own. That would have been OK except that a crisis blew up with my child from my first marriage. I suddenly found myself plunged into a difficult situation, with no Julie, who normally saves me from these things. I didn't know how to cope, I didn't know what to do. I felt so helpless and hopeless. I knew this was beyond me. I felt utterly and overwhelmingly alone. That was it. I could have been in the middle of a packed Wembley Stadium and yet still have only been aware of how alone I was. In the middle of that I said it, "God, if you are there, help!"

'Well, I scraped through that week and all I could think was *I must get to church on Sunday*. I don't know why. I just knew I had to be there. When Julie walked through the door braced to face me after the great time she had had at New Wine, I think it was the first thing I said to her: "Hallo. I'm going to church with you tomorrow."'

'I thought he was winding me up at first. I really didn't believe he meant it, but the next morning there he was, in church with us.'

'Julie was not at my side for long as she was off to the Den Gangs. I was on my own again. This time it was quite incredible. It was like the whole service—songs, Bible readings, sermon—was just for me. God came for me. And that was it. I was in, lock, stock and barrel. From being nothing to me, Jesus was now everything. I jumped straight in the deep end, from nothing to all.'

So you both lived happily ever after?

'Well, no actually! The following year was the hardest ever. Julie found it hard to swallow my swapping leaving threats for Bible quotes.'

'Yes, I didn't believe in what had happened to Keith for ages. Then all this anger came out in me. I was so very angry with him for all he had put me through. He was extremely sorry, but that didn't help. I was cross with God too—I had struggled so hard and it had been so easy for Keith. It sounds ridiculous, but I also found it hard that I suddenly had to share Jesus with him. Jesus was *my* best friend after all. So I had to vent, and he had to accept what he had done. All the pretence in our relationship vanished. The honesty which replaced it was painful—as if God swept away all our lives had been based on and left us dangling in mid-air, clinging to him because there was nothing else. But we talked and talked, and gradually God put in his foundation stones, his bricks.

'For a while, our Christian lives ran parallel, not touching, but we worked through to realise and understand our character differences, to pray together, and to recognise that we are in the same race.

'We have both had to learn such different things along the way. Keith spent the first year of his Christian life apologising to everyone else as well as me. He made the mistake of asking God to soften his heart towards others. So he's doing counselling and Bible study courses. I have had to work out my identity in Christ and fight to let go of my independent capable streak. I've gradually realised that God is bigger than me. He is big enough to cope with all that I give him, big enough to give me a reason for living beyond the daily routines.'

So has it been worth the struggle?

'Oh yes! Though it is a process, isn't it? But we are on the road—and no, we wouldn't go back!'

That is what it is all about!

Having a church building of our own also enabled us to pursue some community-minded ideas that had been brewing for a while. Dave and Janet set up a Drop In on Thursday mornings, with coffee, chat and a whole stack of Social Service leaflets on every subject under the sun. There was room to run a Community Share Scheme for any who would benefit, where all who could donate extra groceries did, in order that those who needed it could help themselves. This was well used for a good time.

However, our little triangle of land in the middle of Cavendish Park was by no means forgotten. On the contrary, we wanted to push ahead. It was still our first commitment. One problem arose as we anticipated returning tenders. Because we were in a part of an existing parish, yet were not a daughter church, we did not actually legally exist. This was clearly something of an anomaly which needed attention, despite causing much amusement. Together with John Cull we drew up an agreement to become a conventional district (a parish in a parish). We could now officially own the ninety-nine year lease for the site. It was ours.

So we were empowered to act when the tenders came in but had to ask the question again. Did we need a building on Cavendish Park?

'Yes. The estates need to see that God is alive—a church building represents that.'

We were unanimous on that one. But which design? Should it be the glorified barn? Or that long low structure? Or that one which looks more like a traditional church? What do we need inside? How many toilets? Room for an office? What about the Den Gangs? What future uses do we envisage?

But as we studied the plans together, one seemed to be more popular. The almost L-shaped design had been submitted by a Bristol-based company. It looked promising. The worship area had an eye-catching diamond-shaped roof, with room inside for 220 seats, a baptistry, store room and crèche. The foyer led off at an angle, with kitchen, meeting rooms, toilets, and office on either side. The entrance was glazed and attractive. Was this it, our new building? Tentatively we pursued the possibility.

We discovered just how protracted the building business

could be, with surveys, planning permission (already obtained in outline) and letters galore. As the year progressed however, problems began to multiply. The original estimate had been for our acceptable figure—£300,000—but as preliminary discussions grew more detailed, the figure began creeping up, while the floor space on the plans kept shrinking.

Trying to solve this became increasingly complicated and headaches abounded. Graham battled to find a way through. Where had it all gone wrong? Letters sped back and forth, phone calls proliferated, but even a face-to-face meeting could not clear up the mess. We were very concerned about the financial side. Graham decided to test the spiritual waters, so to speak. Operation Gideon's Fleece was announced in July 1992. If we went ahead with the project we would need to find roughly £27,000 each month to pay for it, so the idea was that we would pray for this amount before the September decision time. Two months. Surely God could do this? After all, he had provided £200,000 in a single phone call. So we prayed, we gave, we explored fund-raising ideas. We had a Gift Day which resulted in a miserable £240. The weeks ticked away. We raised a little more. I kept expectng a miracle, like last time. Right up to the last minute, I looked for something spectacular.

You guessed. It did not happen.

It did not make sense. Wasn't this the 'right' building? Hadn't we all agreed? Well, all except one, I think. He had always felt that the building looked too much like a railway station, and that the company was based too far away for practicalities. But Ivan had graciously accepted the vastly majority view and worked with it willingly. Now I remembered that he had never voted for it. His insights now faced their biggest challenge as Graham invited him to take over the steering of the building project.

'I just cannot afford the time any more, Ivan. The rest of our church's life is getting neglected. Will you do it?'

So Ivan braced himself. Eventually we felt compelled to call a halt to the proceedings with the Bristol company. It was hard to understand. We had lost the best part of a year barking up the wrong tree. There had been so much hard work on all sides, and there was nothing to show for it except a protracted wrangle with the company over fees incurred, which solicitors had to disentangle.

It was all very dispiriting, but here we were, literally back at the drawing board. Thank goodness for St Philip's. At least we did not have the nomadic pressure as well. In fact, St Philip's was proving an excellent home, and we were very settled there. It needed a lot of maintenance, which was a trial for our churchwardens, but generally was serving us well.

Out of the blue, a letter came from the Ingram Smith building company, one of our previous tendering firms. They had heard, goodness knows how, that we were back in the business of looking for a building. Ivan suggested we give them another chance. Warily, contact was made.

Could this be it? Would we have success this time? I hardly dared to hope. Our experience dictated caution; but it was heartening to discover that the architect, David Summers, was a Christian himself. When Ivan told him we needed adequate space for children's work, for meeting together, for prayer—he understood. Ivan stressed we wanted to make best use of our plot of land and he took that on board. There was much to-ing and fro-ing of paper as he designed and modified in conjunction with Ivan and Graham, but finally there was a design to put before the church. Price tag? £338,000. Guaranteed.

It was time for another day of prayer. November now. The suggested plans were displayed. It has to be said, they were imaginative and impressive showing an octagonal building set into the 'fat' end of our triangular land, making full use of every centimetre yet still leaving room for both limited expansion and the legally-required car parking facilities. It was a partially two-storey design with a central apex, topped by a cross, allowing for a large worship area and also kitchen, toilets, office and crèche on the ground floor, plus two small and one large meeting rooms on the second with another toilet and corridor. A final stroke of genius was the little access bridge from the second storey to the steeply inclining pavement and road beyond, dispensing with the need for a lift and making the top storey independent if necessary. It was an attractive overall design of brick and glass, toning with the surrounding houses, yet distinct from them. A little fenced-in garden leading from the crèche finished it off.

'Hey, that looks good!'

'It is hard to imagine on paper, but it really does look promising.'

'I see we could arrange the 220 seats in the worship area in different ways. It's pretty versatile.'

'The upstairs corridor internal windows will look over the worship room, rather like a balcony.'

'There will be room in the foyer for having teas and coffees; it could be very welcoming.'

'I like the porch at the front. It looks very open and inviting. All the glass helps that too.'

If we were to build, this had to be it. We settled to discussion, prayer, food (of course) and thought. We had the plans to decide on, and also the question of what to do with St Philip's. Ivan and Ann, who were very committed to the area, did not want to abandon it, so the vision for the future became two-fold.

'Not only do we want to build, but when we move to the new building, we will leave a congregation here at St Philip's, in effect planting a new congregation in this area. Please consider all this carefully and prayerfully. We will indicate responses at the evening meeting.'

It must have been a powerful day. Fifty-eight church members indicated definite responses. For example:

'I feel it is now time to take a further step in faith, but putting our trust in God to allow this vision to come about. We have seen what God has done in the last three and a half years, it is time to allow God's kingdom to be advanced on Cavendish Park.

'As far as I can tell I am sure God is in this project. As you know I am very cautious by nature.'

'There is an urgent need for a building. I felt a great sense of peace. I felt the Lord saying, "I affirm you, I affirm your project."'

'While praying, I was standing with my hands out and I felt the Lord push them together saying "Together" over and over. I felt he was saying we will achieve this together.'

There were doubts however:

'I feel that to abstain is my only option. Financially, as a church the time is not right. How can we take on debt? How can we put pressure on people to give money when so many are already struggling?'

'It is a wonderful project, but in the present recession is it possible?'

'I cannot share the vision if it includes a proposal to keep St Philip's open as a church as well.'

Final count? Fifty-five for, three uncertain. No 'no's'! I guess the ideal is that if we are all in touch with the same

Holy Spirit we should be unanimous, but it was the best we could do.

2nd December 1992. The letter was written. We were having another go at building for CCC. Would it work out this time?

10

The Real Thing

Some might say that it is far easier to pin-point gaps in community life than to plug them. Over the last few years, the Cavendish Community Church has been aiming to find and fill some of these gaps and our latest initiative is the most ambitious yet.

On a small piece of land made available to us by Trinity College we are planning a new development that we hope will be a real boost to our community life. The community church building will put a visible new spiritual heart in the community—a place for worship, prayer, study and fun.

It will also be a place of meeting and welcome for all. Not just on Sundays but during the week too, developing a range of activities for local residents of all ages. It will be a place where you can call in for a coffee, or join in with sound educational or recreational activities. Hopefully it will also be a place where you can bring your spiritual searching and meet our living God who through Jesus reaches out to fill all the gaps in our lives.

So ran the hopeful blurb written by my husband. This was our dream. Now we were trying again to turn it into reality. I caught myself almost holding my breath.

I will skip the boring details. There were unbelievable reams of nit-picking questions which Ivan and Castons (chartered surveyor) fired at Ingram Smith; revised drawings after revised drawings; surveys of us all to trawl priorities for the building's use; final planning permission; ground testings. I had had no idea how much was involved. Ivan refused to be shaken off the smallest detail and his tenacity was rewarded. Finally he had plans to our satisfaction. It was September 1993 and the tender was officially accepted. There was no going back now.

Meanwhile, there was the question of the money. For Ivan this was the difficult bit:

> I have to admit that I found the money side hard. I liked the design immensely but could not see where the pounds were going to come from. We were a congregation of only just over 100, many new Christians, many already struggling financially. I just could not see us coping. Graham seemed to be the one with the vision for it, so I said to him, 'I'll do the bricks and mortar, but you look after the pounds and pence.'

Well, we had the promise from Trinity College and the diocese, bless them. That still left £140,000 to find, plus £10,000 to Castons and £20,000 for equipping the finished church. That was all! Peter Livey headed up the Building Fund and swung into action with copious literature to absolutely anyone who might be interested in supporting us:

> At work I often dealt with large sums of money, having to make snap decisions involving chartering ships and so on. I had also experienced God as provider in my own life. As far as I was concerned, God had confirmed that it was his will for there to be a church on Cavendish Park, and I was absolutely sure that the creator of the universe didn't have a problem with releasing funds for his project. So I put together a leaflet and spent many nights into the wee hours with my

wife and others in our congregation folding and stapling countless numbers of them which we sent to local businesses, to the top 500 UK companies and trusts which we knew gave charitably. The initial results were quite underwhelming. After all this hard work, there was not much to show for it. There was some welcome support from our local Barclays Bank and Felixstowe Town Council, the Rank Foundation and the OOCL shipping company. But that was it. However, this was at the stage when our first building plans also fell through, so it was back to basics all round.

As the new plans with Ingram Smith went ahead, Peter produced a specially designed leaflet for the Cavendish Park estates, partly to communicate our aim and partly to invite contributions. It included an artist's impression by David Griggs of what our new church would look like, explanations of what we were up to, a prayer and even a piece from Bishop John Dennis, who wrote:

> Much to many people's surprise the truth is that more churches are being built in England than are being closed. They open as new areas are built up so that the people of the area who wish to worship God and serve him by serving the community have a place to do it in and from.
>
> The time is ripe now for such a building on Cavendish Park. Plans have been laid. The community will benefit enormously in many ways and the church will grow.
>
> The venture has my very strong backing and support. I hope it will have yours.

Meanwhile, Peter and wife Liz bombarded half the world requesting prayer for our project; Paul Yonggi Cho's church in Korea did not escape, nor Dawn Congress, nor most of Scotland and churches in England, Ireland and Malta.

'Leaflets were sent to churches all over the place. We were asking for prayer first and money second,' said

Peter. 'I think more time was spent keeping people informed of what to pray for than we spent in raising money. I also tried to keep the local press informed of developments all the way through and they gave us quite a bit of sympathetic coverage.'

We were doing our own praying, of course. Perhaps if there had still been only twenty of us, it would have been more obvious that each of us was personally responsible. But it is so easy to assume that everyone else is carrying the can and it took a while for the penny to drop. Or rather pennies. It was a huge growth point for the church as we gradually realised the part each one had to play that no one else could. Slowly the covenant forms began to be filled in. If we want it, we have to pay for it. Perhaps we had been cushioned against financial realities by the generosity of our fellow Anglicans, still supporting us even now. Graham was still a free minister for CCC. It also seems that God has his own way of shaking up our purses. It was fascinating that he had, through CCC's Forum, asked Pete Livey to deal with the Building Fund. Hear Liz's story:

It is an amazing adventure unfolding before my eyes. I look back in wonder to where we have been.

I was brought up in a council estate in Lanarkshire, Scotland. My memories of money were of savings stamps, the 'Prudential' man calling each week, and saving for holidays once a year. We paid our dues and only spent what we had. My parents didn't earn a lot, and it was not until I took my first Saturday job that I had my own money. I discovered that money could buy luxuries like clothes and travel. It also bought treats for my parents, especially when Dad retired through ill health. Yet I think it also brought me a warped sense of control, as if it could change me into whatever I wanted.

Then I married Peter in September 1981. His family had their own home, a car, a caravan and horse. It was all so different from the upbringing I had known. So of course we bought our own flat. It was a bargain and lovely, but looking back I see the millstone appearing. We had no savings for the work it needed and the mortgage, but I soon got used to the constant overdraft. Well, everybody did it. We then moved to a bigger house. So the money problem got bigger too, but the good bit was that it was at this time that my love for the Lord was rekindled. I had lived as a believer before, but now God became very real to me. I rejoined a living church and found the Lord again, not that *he* had ever been away. Within sixteen months we had moved south to a different culture and more financial worries.

It was boom time in the 1980s and everything was vastly overpriced. We had a smaller, more expensive home with new furniture, poll tax, water tax, and so on. I started to go to a local church of good people, but none of them seemed to have money worries, and I didn't feel I belonged. To make matters worse, Peter remained a committed atheist. Then we had our first daughter, which meant I lost my wage at the time Peter had gone into a salaried managerial job. We lost £13,000 a year in earnings. It was a downward spiral then. It broke my heart when I had to find part-time work when my daughter was only ten months old. I blamed Peter for not looking after his family, something my father had always done. Like some hungry monster demanding to be fed we were having to pay bill after bill. Overdrafts, credit cards, loans—always robbing Peter to pay Paul. I felt my security slip away, along with dignity, respect and motivation. In their place came guilt, fear and unhappiness.

Meanwhile I had joined CCC. I could not talk to anyone about the dreaded subject. It was taboo. Then a breakthrough happened in 1990. My husband got chicken pox. During the three weeks he was off he started to read the Bible to disprove it. A year and much study later he gave himself to the Lord.

Joy unbounded you may think. No way. I was still blaming

him for our constant financial crises, even though we both now loved the Lord. Peter became a steady leader in the church and was then made the Building Fund chairman. I was staggered, but he was elated. For me it was a reminder of our failure; for Peter it was the chance to increase God's work. So with this challenge before us, we decided at this point to walk out of our debt with God's help. We had tried to do it many times on our own. We made a promise to God, but felt his response went something like, 'This won't be easy. You have to be taught about money, to learn how to manage it.'

During this period many ironies took place. We aided others to get out of debt, we sat alongside people with debt crises, we delivered CCC Community Share Scheme items, and even used it ourselves. We worked hard for the Building Fund. Others were solving their debt problems, but we weren't. It seemed so unfair.

At the church houseparty in January 1993, things came to a head for me. It was horrible, I felt I had this ugly creature sitting on my shoulders taunting me about our debts, our giving, the whole thing. I knew if we could clear our £500 overdraft we could start making headway into the rest, but there was no way of doing it. Then one service we sang, 'Jehovah Jireh, my provider, his grace is sufficient for me.' My eyes turned to slits, I couldn't sing, I was blazing angry and biting my tongue. How dare God claim that? How could it be true? No, no, no. I've had it, Jehovah Jireh indeed!

A few days later an envelope was dropped through our door. It came from a dear Christian lady. Enclosed was a greetings card. She had been praying for us as a family and the Lord had told her to give us a sum of money and a message: 'He is Jehovah Jireh, your provider.' With it was £500.

After that we slowly but surely climbed out of our financial pit. I learnt that nothing is impossible for God, and that we cannot walk in true freedom until our purses also sing God's tune, not our own. The last great bastion, the purse. We gave the lot to God and he was faithful.

Peter felt it was important that there was no overnight miracle for them:

> After we confessed to each other and to God the wrong things we had done, most of which were mine, a lot of the tensions disappeared. It may seem crazy but we started to pray together over all the account books, and the picture started to change. We began to believe in God as our provider. As each little crisis arose, we somehow had enough to cope—just in time. I have learned how to be a good steward for my family. If there had been a quick fix, I would not have learnt how to look after them. This year, for the first time, I'll be able to tithe to my church.

Back to the Building Fund. Was Peter's faith paying off? The diocese and Trinity College had agreed to pay the first bills when they came, but recommended that we should not sign anything until we had £275,000 in the coffers. There was the promised £200,000 but only £24,500 otherwise. While investigating loan options, Pete led some fund-raising enthusiasts from the church into a brainstorming session as to what we could do for ourselves. The coming months were to see a variety of events, ranging from the expected, like a Fun Day on the green which netted £500, to the unusual, like the Open Air Gig held on the same. Or perhaps that was not so unexpected—you ought to know them by now. So there was the Sponsored Bike Ride, a Christmas Fayre in the borrowed Trinity Methodist Church, the New Year Barn Dance, the collecting of foil (before the bottom dropped out of that particular market) and cans. We sold bricks— £1 each and a certificate to prove it, which proved very popular with friends and families. We multiplied our talents, taking the £5 provided in an envelope and turning it into jam to sell, or marmalade or fudge or wine. We tried to make all the fundraising fun-raising as well, not just for

us but for any in the community who joined in. We also gave away a percentage of our efforts, in a gesture of gratitude to the God who was providing.

Peter was an unflagging encourager:

> I had been given a brilliant piece of advice by our then curate, Yvonne Irvine, who said to me, 'Keep up the vision, enthuse people about this continuously—oh, and ignore whatever the vicar is promoting at the time!' So I did. We set about explaining and enlisting covenants, and Gift Aid, and made it possible for folks to give interest-free loans.

Gradually the bank balance was creeping up. There were some wonderful moments along the way, such as when the Methodist church round the corner offered to buy us an altar, two lecterns and a table when the building was up. There was also the day when we learned that the diocese were not in a position to underwrite a loan for us . . . then we were offered an interest-free one of £50,000 from another source! With trembling knees at Forum we committed ourselves to the loan, Andrew Rayner reminding us that we might as well go for it, as it would need just as much faith if we waited another six months. Just as important were the children who donated pocket money and the letters which arrived containg the money individuals or churches could spare together with so much warmth and support. The entire Disabled Club meeting in St Philip's bought a brick each. It was very moving to be on the receiving end of such generosity, no matter what the amount.

By September we had our £275,000.

Liz was a churchwarden at the time, along with Steve. On 11th October 1993, together with Graham, they signed the plans and building could commence. If we did not come up with the goods, those two could be financially liable. Would this be why they are both so gifted at praying?

12th October 1993. Bishop John Dennis blessed and consecrated our land, taking the first chunks out of the soil with the aid of a JCB. The mayor took a turn too.

18th October. Ingram Smith took possession of our triangle. It was beginning at last. It was such a relief. No longer did I have to avert my eyes as I trailed across the road to the shop. It was really happening. Yes, there was still lots more money to find, but our little blob of land was finally seeing some action. Now there was nothing sweeter than to detour whenever I went out, to see what was happening. I wanted it built in a week. I could stand by our erstwhile fallow field and feel excitement, joy, hope.

Not that the emotions stopped there. We also had sleepless nights, then dreams of churchwardens in gaol, a vital room forgotten, no money at the end of the month. Daylight and. . . .

The foundations were what? Not in the right place you say? Why not? What pipe was in the way? Why didn't you know about it? Because there are two different measurements to the site boundary. I see. So which is the right one? The council and Graham will have to decide? Six feet did you say? Six feet out? Are you sure? Yes, well yes. We have talked to the council. We are going to split the difference. We will have three feet extra, they will have three feet less. Yes, yes. We can see it is going to work out all right. Just don't do it again.

Why is there a problem with the roof? We want that glass lantern on the top, with the cross . . . no, no we want the original design. . . .

This time it was Ivan who put a spanner in the works.

'That cross with its parallel metal design . . . won't the wind whistle through it? I can just imagine how pleased the neighbours will be with that. Another idea please.'

How does he think of these things?

Yet the excitement mounted with the progress. It was great to wander over the road and watch as huge steel girders were manœuvred into position, clanging metal on metal, building higher, as yellow hard-hatted workers eased the puzzle into place.

But the money battle was not yet over. By November, Peter was producing graphs by the dozen showing our projected shortfall. By January, we knew there was not enough to complete the building. We were aiming for bankruptcy in a couple of months. Horrified gasps greeted his pronouncement, but Peter was unperturbed:

> Each month it got more exciting for me to see what God would do as our funds disappeared. I'm not sure everyone shared this enthusiasm. I also knew that we were finally taking prayer seriously ourselves, and that the Ladies' Prayer Group recently set up for Tuesday nights was praying

consistently for the funds. I felt my back was covered if you like. The first answer seemed to be a Gift Day.

We negotiated with Peter, our patient site manager, for a Saturday in February when the hard-hat rule was relaxed and we could meet together in the shell of our very own church to pray, to sing, to fill it with praise to God right from the beginning. It was stunning to realise it was coming into being at last, right before our eyes, but we needed the finances or we would never realise our dream. Four members of CCC were away this weekend at a prayer conference in Birmingham. While there they prayed and felt the Lord say that £25,000 would be given that day. Bearing in mind our Gift Day of last year which had been such a non-event, this was rather ambitious. But it was a good day here in Felixstowe and by the end we had £25,000 either promised or given, and with reclaimed tax from the covenants it would eventually exceed £30,000. Jehovah Jireh!

There were still some surprises though. One of them was when we prayed and voted for where to go when the building was up, into it or staying at the St Philip's plant. Nearly everyone wanted to move to the new CCC. There was only a handful for St Philip's. It was not enough. After our experience, there was no way we would set up a new church without a decent team. We prayed more, we talked. We prayed again. We asked God for fifteen people, and we did not get them. We were forced to accept that our two-fold vision was not yet viable. The Barleys felt this especially keenly, as they were to have headed up the venture. However, it was not to be at this stage. Yet the vision did not go away, so we chose to wait and see whether it is the time scale we had wrong.

Despite the excitement and commitment of the recent Gift Day, we were still short of the necessary capital to finish our new church. Peter was still enjoying the suspense, but Graham felt that we had asked all we could of our faithful CCC-ites, and yelled to the diocese for help. Although we knew they were strapped for cash themselves, they somehow managed to find us a grant of £30,000 and a loan for the same. Our covenants would cover the repayments and Peter could justifiably wear a large grin. Our prayers were answered. The church would be finished. Our dream would come true.

'So Ivan, how do you feel about the money coming in after all? Wasn't this the hard bit for you?'

'Well, yes. I suppose I find it quite encouraging really.'

He always was the master of understatement.

Meanwhile both he and Graham were still up to their necks in the building anyway, as they and Castons gave many hours to decisions on everything from the type of breeze block to the quality of bolts and screws. As the brickwork crawled up the height of the steel pillars, and the glass of the many windows was steadily set in place, there were many times I found myself holding my breath as I watched the progress. Could it really be happening, after all this time?

A little team was set up to decide colour schemes, not just for kitchen flooring and toilet fixtures, but baptistry tiles and wood stain. It was a terrifying responsibility, because we knew we would not please everybody.

'The carpet has come!'

'Oh great, how does it look?'

'Well, I thought you chose a mixed browns with a hint of red. . . .'

'We did. Why?'

'It is pink.'

'PINK! It can't be the right one. Pink! Let me look. . . .'

But it was. A two-centimetre square section was indeed

WE LISTENED CAREFULLY
TO EVERYBODY
    BEFORE WE BUILT IT

a mix of browns and red, to tone in with the planned paintwork on the ceiling girders, but the effect of the whole area was definitely pink. Metres and metres of it. We had ordered it, and we would have to make the best of it.

Most significant was the day when the seven-metre solid steel cross was swung up into the air on a crane and carefully fixed into place, right on the top. No whistling in the wind, but rather that awful symbol of torture and death raised to the highest point on the estates to proclaim life to our community.

11

Open Air to Opening Day

To return to the black lump. We had our balcony of sorts, the picture that we had had all those years ago was of being able to look down over the congregation. That we certainly could do through the long thin windows set strategically down the first-floor corridor. Indeed, as the building was nearing completion, and we hosted a children's day specially for them to get the feel of their new home-to-be, my eldest declared that the best bits were 'The windows! Great for spying on the grown-ups.'

She had obviously picked up the larger spiritual vision.

What about the lump? I thought it had been a mistake, a flight of fancy from all that fasting. Then the contractors finished off the apex of the roof. What I hadn't realised was that the final covering was black. There is no doubt that the roof of our building is a black lump. It was quite a startling thought. God really *does* know the end from the beginning, just like he says. It is tremendously encouraging too. He will speak to us if we will listen.

However, he does not always seem bothered about the

details. Things started to heat up a little. Peter Livey was working overtime on the finances, Ivan, Graham and Castons were attempting to iron out the inevitable wrinkles in design and timing. But God did not seem to be speaking about all the little decisions—is this why we argue about them so easily in church life?

I suppose it was an emotional stage for us all. We all had some kind of investment in the new building, whether spiritually, financially or both, and I suppose we all wanted to be involved. We all had different ideas about how the finished product should look, and bang! Warts were showing all over the place. Did the children of Israel squabble over the land of Canaan? It would be nice to think of us all pulling happily together but I should have known by now that life does not always work like that. After all, we have been striving for years to be real with each other. Some of this particular slice of reality was painful, but not very different from how it has been all the way along, God working things together anyway, through us or despite us, blessing us even with our warts and the shameful way we treat each other at times. Harsh words were said, tempers lost, yet the building work continued. Then again, sometimes the fellowship we experienced together during this preparation time was great. With all the highs and lows, the building was still advancing.

It was a bit of an intense time anyway. There was so much to be done to be ready and open. The whole place had to be checked by a multitude of officials, including the fire officer who demanded we change the glass on the stairwell to fire-safety regulation, and alter all the locks for proper escape access. It was frustrating. So why had the right glass not been designated originally?

There was the curtain surround for our built-in OHP

screen, which when installed looked like a rather tasteless cinema and totally dominated the worship area and had to be cut down and altered.

There were the prominent steel girders which spanned the interior ceiling of the worship area. Ivan boldly recommended turning their eyesore potential into an eye-catching feature, so we had them painted flame red. It worked.

There was the inside breeze-block brick work which resembled a factory wall. What could we do? A couple of coats of matching magnolia, and the effect was transformed.

We had the burgundy OHP surround, flame girder paint, and background curtain to the dais, red chair coverings and a pink carpet—it was either glorious or gently ghastly, depending on your view of colour.

We bought cream crockery for the kitchen but forgot the kettle. At least that was easily remedied.

Some things went satisfyingly well, like the bins and accessories which were available in *just* the right colours; and the folding tables which proved their worth from the first.

The time ticked on.

We worked out a plan for the run-up to open day, trying to cover the gardening, the kitchen, the carpets, the office, the PA, the deliveries, and moving from St Philip's. It was to be not just activity but prayer as well, with slots arranged to cover the entire range of the church's life. Sometimes enough of us turned up, sometimes not. Concern and frustration clashed with joy and excitement as we struggled on through the list.

The bishop landed in the middle of it all, for a tour round the nearly finished building which was on his itinerary for the visiting Bishop of Hasalt and three other clergy from Belgium. They were all wonderfully encouraging of the design and workmanship, the bishop dubbing our foyer cloisters (coffee in the cloisters!), and admiring our lantern in the apex of the black lump roof.

'How are you going to clean those windows in the lantern?' he asked. 'Oh I shouldn't have asked such an impossible question. Perhaps I'd better do it myself.'

What more could one ask in a diocesan bishop?

A week before our opening and we finally held the keys in our hands. It was 3rd June 1994. Ivan and Castons had exhausted their list of outstanding defects, the finishing touches were under control and there was nothing to delay for any more. We took a few photos with long-suffering site manager Peter, and we had done it. It was not yet the official handover, but to all intents and purposes the building was now complete and ours. Graham was so overwhelmed he retired to the bath. I think I recoursed to the teapot. Then it was back to the list of things still to be done.

Many exhaustions later, a week to be precise, it was official reception day.

The church looked lovely, decorated with flowers and banners, and ready for the visitors—builder's representatives, architect, CCC-ites, sponsors—to gather, hear the obligatory speeches of appreciation and tour the building. The upper room rose to the challenge of its first catering opportunity, and we all struggled with disbelief that we had just made it in time.

It was incredible that the bricks and mortar for which we had prayed, worked and dreamed were actually being used for the first time as a building. I could not concentrate at all on the official proceedings. I assume they were good. I just kept looking round at all those windows in the worship area, low ones showing the green bank beyond, high ones the blue soaring sky. Then up, past the flame paint on the steel girders, to the slanted glass of the central lantern, through which the towering cross was visible. Then all the lovely wood caught my eye; walnut-tinted window surrounds, light oak doors. The ash-wood chairs, as many as we could afford, with their guardsman-red coloured padding. Windows through to the foyer, windows out to the porch—windows everywhere. Light poured in, bouncing off the brass fittings, highlighting the soft oak of the new altar and lectern. Walking upstairs for the reception, past all those toilets, peering down through the spy windows, I still couldn't believe it was real. The green-carpeted upper room seemed larger than ever, the full-length windows offering a fascinating view over the houses and away across the estuary. Yes, it was good.

The really big day, however, was Sunday when we had our first worship service in our new CCC family home. It was just for us, the guest service was next week. 170 of us were there, all a little tense, overwhelmed at arriving across our 'Jordan' at last. Finally it was a chance to worship the God who had promised five years ago: 'I will build my church.' It was hard to know where to look, as all the unfamiliar shapes and colours attracted the eye. Ivan captured our attention with a stirring sermon on crossing the Jordan and the bigger battles yet to come. The children were as high as kites with excitement, a far more appropriate reaction than feeling overwhelmed. Hardly had Graham uttered the magic words, 'Now it is time for Den Gangs,' when there was a delighted rush for the door and upstairs. Apparently the time went well—all survived with smiles intact. The lovely big kitchen made serving drinks after the service easy, and there was a real buzz around. It seemed the building had surpassed all our expectations and hopes. Yet there was also a sense of unreality. It was hard to take in that the dream had come true. We indulged in a shared lunch upstairs, and discovered immediately that the dumb-waiter had its limitations—a full load of cups and saucers were too much and it promptly broke. It all seemed such a far cry from scrabbling in our home kitchen to find enough mugs, a very long journey ago. Here I was, gazing out over a third of Felixstowe to the docks and river beyond. Was it really happening?

There was little opportunity for reflection, though, as we dived into a crazy fortnight of hospitality events, to give all and sundry a chance to come and look, and for some to begin to feel at home. We held a communion service for our elderly and disabled friends (including those from Reynolds Court), a children's welcome party, a men's breakfast for church members and guests, an evening social for family, friends and neighbours, coffee and worship for local Christians from other churches, a town ministers' get together, plus open coffee mornings on the Tuesday and Thursday which proved so popular we kept them going after the fortnight. With sweet peas gracing the tables, and a toy corner for the children, it looked welcoming. We must have had about sixty people through the doors each time. Young mums and their toddlers, senior folk and others wanting to have a look. So I was one of a team who showed them round, enjoyed the appreciation and hoped they would come back.

'There is so much room.'

'It is so beautifully light.'

'The garden is great.'

'I love it that you have so many toilets.'

Also:

'Where does the choir stand?'

We do not have one. Or:

'They have not fitted the carpet very well here.'

We were standing on the removable boards on top of the baptistry. This latter was revealed many times during those two weeks, as visitors were invited to view the shark mosaic on the bottom. (No, there wasn't!)

I think we all felt better once the carpet had had its first spills as well—we relaxed and churchwarden Keith stopped retorting, 'Not on my carpet!'

Yet amid all the hustle and bustle, the packing up after each event and preparing for the next, there was a sense of peace that hit me every time I walked through the doors. Not just because it was a lovely, new clean light and airy building, but because God was there. It felt different, special. Not just an achievement but a promise. A place built in honour of God, Father, Son and Holy Spirit, for him to meet with people there.

The second Sunday was the guest service, the one we advertised. It was packed with about 230 people, children sitting on the floor.

We still had the official dedication to come on 17th July, with special music, symbolic offering of our talents and life to God, and Bishop Jonathan Bailey. But for me, this second Sunday was the big day. The day we came home.

Many of us had invited family members from afar to share the celebration, and there were lots of visitors. It was a glorious day outside and in. There was a buzz of excitement as we gathered, CCC members feeling more at ease than the previous week. It was such a special time. The music was great, the sketch hard hitting, the solo stunning, and the talk excellent (and I am pretty critical of my husband's sermons). It felt to me that it would have been extremely hard to miss the sense of God's presence as we worshipped together and considered the challenge to discover if God is alive, well and interested in us. The sun streamed in the many windows, lighting the worship room up with warmth.

To me it was as if last week had been the false labour and this the birth. There was such a powerful feeling of God's spirit and of joy. I savoured the sweetness of what God had done and felt full to bursting. He is faithful. He does keep his word. He has done it. Totally brilliant. We had arrived. We had made it.

Made it? What am I saying? Have I forgotten so soon? Just at this moment, this innovative structure means so much to me, yet it is merely a shell, a symbol. I, of all people, should have learnt by now that it really is not the building that counts, but the people. It is the people God loves, people he draws together. None of this would have happened without that, without them. I still do not understand it any more than when we started, why it is that this one hears his voice and responds and that one does not seem to. I know it is something to do with prayer and obedience and welcome and openness, but it has to be God. It is not us. It is he who changes lives. Incredibly it is he who wants relationship with wayward, warty us. It is this reality that counts. Otherwise we might as well not have come.

And now? Five years down the line from a pink lounge and trembling hearts? Now is just the beginning.

Postscript

Cavendish Community Church is still a growing church. If you would like to contact us, our address is:

Cavendish Community Church
Grange Farm Avenue
Felixstowe
IP11 8FB